MASS APPEAL

MASS APPEAL

Communicating Policy Ideas in Multiple Media

JUSTIN GEST

OXFORD
UNIVERSITY PRESS

Oxford University Press is a department of the University of Oxford. It furthers the University's objective of excellence in research, scholarship, and education by publishing worldwide. Oxford is a registered trade mark of Oxford University Press in the UK and certain other countries.

Published in the United States of America by Oxford University Press
198 Madison Avenue, New York, NY 10016, United States of America.

Library of Congress Cataloging-in-Publication Data
Names: Gest, Justin, author.
Title: Mass appeal : communicating policy ideas in multiple media / Justin Gest.
Description: New York, NY : Oxford University Press, [2020] |
Includes bibliographical references and index.
Identifiers: LCCN 2019056312 (print) | LCCN 2019056313 (ebook) |
ISBN 9780190062170 (hardback) | ISBN 9780190062187 (paperback) |
ISBN 9780190062200 (epub)
Subjects: LCSH: Communication in politics—United States. |
Political planning—United States. | Persuasion (Rhetoric) in mass media.
Classification: LCC JA85.2.U6 G47 2019 (print) | LCC JA85.2.U6 (ebook) |
DDC 320.97301/4—dc23
LC record available at https://lccn.loc.gov/2019056312
LC ebook record available at https://lccn.loc.gov/2019056313

9 8 7 6 5 4 3 2 1

Paperback printed by LSC Communications, United States of America
Hardback printed by Bridgeport National Bindery, Inc., United States of America

Wherever the people are well informed they can be trusted with their own government.

LETTER FROM THOMAS JEFFERSON TO RICHARD PRICE

PARIS, *8 January 1789*

CONTENTS

FOREWORD

Silence.

I was a 27-year-old recent PhD graduate who spent the last decade as a newspaper reporter and television production freelancer. I had just published a book on one of the most divisive, misunderstood populations in the Western world. Yet the reaction to it can be summarized in one word: silence. No phone calls from the UK Home Office or the US State Department soliciting my expertise. No inspired efforts by civil society organizations. No newspaper columns debating my most controversial ideas.

I had spent six months fully immersed in Muslim communities in London and Madrid, shortly after each city had been rocked by terrorist attacks that killed and injured hundreds of people and inspired a wave of Islamic extremism. Using my investigative journalism skills, I had managed to interview members of an extremist organization and take notes during their meetings. I had invested countless hours over a three-year period, researching Western

Muslim politics and writing up my findings. I even had a stylized book jacket that friends likened to a movie poster. The whole package was published by a highly reputable press in the thick of rampant Islamophobia, paranoia about Islamic extremism, and unease about immigration into Europe and the United States. As far as research goes for a social scientist, I thought I had struck gold.

And yet silence. My then novel policy ideas of embracing mosques as partners in anti-terrorism strategies; of eliminating random Muslim profiling, stop-and-search and other discriminatory enforcement tactics; and of focusing terrorism prevention on second-generation, immigrant-origin Muslims frustrated by democracy and concerned with the development of their identity all seemed to fall on deaf ears.

Suddenly, I was the one who was frustrated with democracy. Where was its meritocracy? Where were the channels open to new ideas and voices? Where was the public desire for reform? Why was nobody listening? At first, I was resigned to accept the advice I might have otherwise shared with my alienated subjects: democracy is flawed, and sometimes your ideas become lost in the crowd.

However, I also knew that democracy is highly subject to our ability to inject our personal preferences into public discourse—broadly, strategically, and effectively. And upon reflection, I failed to use many of the skills I gained during my years as a journalist. Experiences in print, radio, and television journalism taught me how to communicate to broad and diverse audiences and readerships. And yet, I never really employed those skills as well as I could have to communicate the ideas I developed from a book project that required far more effort than any article I had ever written for a newspaper.

Determined not to let this happen again, I dedicated myself to integrating these skills to share my future research—to communicate my policy ideas effectively in multiple media. I now use them all the time in order to ensure that every major piece of research I undertake can be consumed and understood by academics, policymakers, and the public alike. And along the way, I have encountered many other public policy professionals—researchers as well as activists, advocates, bureaucrats, and officials—who shared my earlier frustrations and wanted to broaden their reach as well.

Public policy education and training are oriented around the development of critical and innovative ideas about how to improve governance and make society better. However, they undervalue one of the most important tools needed to translate policy proposals into action: the ability to communicate ideas broadly, strategically, and effectively. This is the primary objective of *Mass Appeal*. This book is a primer for students, researchers, and policy professionals who want to turn their analyses and memos into clear, persuasive campaigns—which may be reporting their findings or advocating a perspective. In politics, rarely do influencers have the time to read tomes about policy. Key decisions are often made on the basis of media campaigns and digestible snippets. It is simply not enough to develop policy ideas: you must be able to distribute them effectively. As Shanto Iyengar and Donald Kinder show in their seminal work *News That Matters*,[1] issues that receive more coverage in the national news become more important to the public. In other words, news media has "agenda-setting" power.

1. Iyengar, S., & Kinder, D. R. (2010). *News that matters: Television and American opinion*. Chicago, IL: University of Chicago Press.

This text is designed as a practical introduction for students and professionals who want their research, analysis, and ideas to hold greater mass appeal but who have limited experience with communications media. For students, the book accompanies broader public policy textbooks that more comprehensively review the state of knowledge about policymaking processes and analysis. For both students and professionals, the book complements the expertise that you have developed over the course of your studies and careers in certain issue areas or industrial sectors. These classroom and workplace experiences prepare us for policy creation, management, and analysis; but they do not offer guidance in the basic products of political communication across multiple media. If you read the chapters that follow and apply the lessons to your own work, you will become more confident in writing succinctly and engaging in public speaking.

Chapter 1 explains the rationale for this book and introduces the indispensability of pithy statements to clear communication. Chapters 2 through 8 each discuss the fundamentals of a specific medium of communication. Structured consistently, they begin with an outline of the **principles** underpinning the medium, its recommended structure, and the nature of its target audience or readership. Each chapter then quotes complementary advice from expert **practitioners** who I specifically commissioned to present their remarks. And finally, each chapter offers examples that are **paragons** of good communication. I focus on examples from the American context, but the lessons are intended to be applicable in the policy environments of other democracies as well. Chapter 9 concludes with sensible criteria for determining what media are most appropriate for reaching different types of policy goals.

Throughout the book, I try to practice what I preach. I try to write succinctly—offering the most essential information, carefully selecting my language for clarity, and striving for mass appeal.

ACKNOWLEDGMENTS

Early in my freshman year at University High School in Los Angeles, I read an article in the school's weekly newspaper that I felt misrepresented the facts behind a school political issue. I was so outraged that I marched to the journalism classroom to approach the paper's advisor, Olga Kokino. Just as I began to share my displeasure, she said brusquely: "Why don't *you* write it next time?"

This started a lifetime interest in reporting, writing, and commentary. Ms. Kokino, who passed away in 2016, embodied the soulful devotion required to teach writing and teach young minds how journalists write in a different language, even though it's still English. She inspired me to learn, to write, and to be myself. She was always as proud of the academic studies I authored as the articles I published on any newspaper's front page.

When I arrived as an undergraduate at Harvard, I immediately joined the campus daily, *The Harvard Crimson*. Harvard has no journalism major. While some assume that journalism is far too practical, too trade-like to be a recognized field of academic study, perhaps faculty know what I was swiftly taught by my most beloved editor, Sugi Ganeshananthan: the best place to learn how to be a reporter is the newsroom; not the classroom.

Over the decade that followed, I wrote as a staff writer, freelancer, and television production assistant, even during my PhD program. I'm not sure if it was a back-up plan, side hustle, or just an addiction; I just loved it and it defined my early development. I covered police brutality, cigarette smoking bans, terrorism, endangered wetlands and, of course, the weather, for many publications and broadcast networks. I interviewed countless celebrities, athletes, political leaders, but also a mother right after her son died in a tragic car accident. I investigated corruption, snuck into private events, and was once thrown onto the hood of a squad car. Through it all, I learned how to write thanks to the precious time many editors and colleagues shared to guide my development, through good and bad. This book is their work too.

I would like to thank David Beard, who rolled the dice on a 20-year-old reporter at *The Boston Globe*; Jon Morosi, Jon Eirich, and John Wolff from my time at WHRB; Michelle Orrego, Marta Waller, and Stan Chambers who embraced me like a son when I interned at KTLA; Elizabeth Wilner and Chris Wallace when I was at ABC News; Joel Havemann, Dick Cooper, Jack Nelson, and Ron Brownstein when I was at the *Los Angeles Times*; Eric Berger, David Ivanovich, Steve Jetton, Samantha Levine, Nancy Martinez, and Julie Mason when I was at the *Houston Chronicle*; Terry Michael, who long ran the Washington Center for Politics & Journalism; Ravi Agrawal, Christiane Amanpour, Becky Anderson, and Nic Robertson when I was at CNN; Alison Silver, my editor when she was at Reuters; and Elizabeth Ralph, my editor at POLITICO. Across all these experiences, Matt Bai, Bill Schneider, Kathy and Ted Gest counselled me, always took my calls, and often took me to lunch.

For so long, it was unclear how my journalistic work would contribute to my scholarly pursuits. However, Steve Levitsky, David Held, and Henrietta Moore embraced that side of my background and encouraged me to leverage it to become a more rigorous scholar and a more effective teacher. I remain forever grateful for their mentorship. At the London School of Economics, I am also indebted to Neil McLean for teaching me how to teach.

This book was originally derived from the lessons in policy communication that I designed and incorporated into the introductory Masters in Public Policy course at George Mason University's Schar School of Policy and Government. I owe so much to my students over the years, and to my faculty peers who assigned early manuscripts of this book and influenced the design of my syllabi. Thank you to Lee Fritschler, Jack Goldstone, Rich Kauzlarich, Jerry Mayer, Steve Pearlstein, Mark Rozell, Cathy Rudder, Sita Slavov, Bonnie Stabile, and the many students who offered their feedback.

This book would not have been possible without the brilliant practitioners who generously contributed their ideas to compliment and supplement my own. I sincerely thank Spencer Boyer, Peter Canellos, Jonathan Capehart, Lyndsay Duncombe, Kathy Gest, Alexandra Sicotte-Levesque, Ralph Mamiya, Paige Reffe, and Bill Schneider. Thank you to Fareed Zakaria who helped facilitate Oxford's license to reproduce content from his CNN show, and for his own willingness to share his guidance over the last few years. Thank you also to Michael Morell and Elise Morrison for imparting their wisdom, which I share in this book.

Thank you to Josh Goldstein, David Lampo, Tim O'Shea, and Andrew Schappert for their assistance in the preparation of this manuscript and its website, MassAppeal.gmu.edu. Thank you to my dear friend, Justin Fraterman, for always being ready for my most random queries. Thank you to my book editor, Angela Chnapko, for her vision, her patience, and for believing in my ideas. I am also grateful for the support of Oxford University Press' Alexcee Bechthold, Dave McBride, and Niko Pfund.

Finally, I am blessed to have such a beautiful, loving family: Max and Gail; Darren and Rebecca; Phillip and Franklin; György and Tanja; Adam and George; Valentina and Hugo; and my extraordinary wife, Monika, whose love—despite my concern with Mass Appeal—is all I really need.

1

A MULTILINGUAL TOOLKIT

WARS OF WORDS

Written text is at the core of almost all products in society. A start-up rests on a business plan. A film is produced according to a screenplay. A new building has a project description. Scientific findings are communicated in lab reports. A ballad is composed of lyrics. Partnerships are based on contracts. Inventions are secured by patents. Diplomacy is grounded in treaties. In every case, the success of each endeavor is largely determined by the style and content of the text that describes or explains it.

Why would public policy and policy campaigns be any different? Policy itself is perhaps more naturally derived from written legislation. It is, after all, law or an interpretation of the law. However, the world of policy cannot be separated from the world of politics, and politics is about persuasion. Accordingly, no matter how ingenious your policy idea is, it is unlikely to attract support or recognition if you are unable to communicate it broadly, strategically, and effectively.

The problem with public policy materials—analyses, platforms, and bills—is that these foundational texts are written to be well referenced, rigorous, and possibly legally binding; they are not written to be broadly read. A small percentage of people have read the Universal Declaration of Human Rights, and yet many will know that equal protection and justice, freedom from discrimination, and freedom from torture and slavery are inalienable human rights. Few people have ever read the Affordable Care Act, but most know it as "Obamacare" and hold a strong opinion about it. In every electoral campaign, candidates and parties prepare platforms and manifestos, and yet very few voters rely on these documents to make their decisions in the voting booth.

Public policy ideas, therefore, require authors and advocates to promote their ideas in the public sphere. Authors and advocates must convert their foundational texts into more appealing, memorable media. These conversions are designed to fit into the informational media that we consume on a daily basis—social media, news articles, television shows, radio broadcasts, briefings, or even casual conversations. In contrast, foundational texts such as the Universal Declaration of Human Rights, the Affordable Care Act, or the Democratic Party platform would never be reproduced or read in any of these media. They would, of course, require too much time or space.

There are three key components to these media conversions, the first of which is the **material**. In political communication, the material content is a matter of clarity of focus and a concern for interpretation. In his (in)famous *Rules for Radicals*, US leftist activist Saul Alinsky featured this idea: "Pick the target, freeze it, personalize it, polarize it."[1] With these words, Alinsky inspired generations of community organizers to agitate by simplifying their messages,

1. Alinsky, Saul D. (1990). *Rules for radicals: A pragmatic primer for realistic radicals*. New York, NY: Vintage Books.

providing sharp contrasts, and applying the cause to people's daily lives. However, even the most well-crafted messages must account for interpretation. US speechwriter Frank Luntz's book on public speaking, *Words That Work* (2007), emphasizes this: "It's not what you say—it's what people hear."[2] Content must be audience-focused, not author-focused.

Second, the text is as much about the **messenger** as it is about the message. Ask yourself, "Why me?" Why should anyone listen to your ideas about climate change? Have you just completed a scientific study on the effect of coal burning on global warming? Have you just authored a government report that provides a cost–benefit analysis of new greenhouse gas regulation? Do you represent a constituency of people from a low-lying island at risk of submersion by rising sea levels? This is your story and the way you generate both interest and credibility. At the same time, it is important that you are not intimidated by the qualifications of others in the debate. Also ask, "Why not me?"

Third, you must select the appropriate **medium** and venue for your message. The attributes of different media lend themselves to communicating different types of messages. A popular view of politics would emphasize the importance of public pressure. However, some subject matters are too obscure for public interest or are decided by unelected arbiters. In these cases, you must address the decision maker directly or identify points of leverage. Another question is whether your message must be nuanced or whether you can be more persuasive by presenting an overview.

2. Luntz, F. (2007). *Words that work: It's not what you say, it's what people hear*. New York, NY: Hachette Books.

MULTILINGUALISM

For this reason, the more media in which you can fluently communicate your message, the more effective you will be. In this way, media are like languages: the more you speak, the more people you may reach. This book offers guidance about seven foundational media in the world of political communication:

Chapter 2	Executive Summaries
Chapter 3	Press Releases
Chapter 4	Op-Eds and Blogs
Chapter 5	Briefings
Chapter 6	Broadcast Appearances
Chapter 7	Elevator Pitches
Chapter 8	Websites and Social Media

Because different causes and campaigns require different strategies, versatility is invaluable. It allows you to adapt to the circumstances and communicate your ideas to address multiple target audiences, each in a way that works for that particular community. Chapter 9 focuses on choosing which medium to engage once you have a better understanding of each.

TOPIC SENTENCES

Topic sentences are the backbone of all written work and each of these media. They are typically understood to be the first sentence in an expository paragraph, summarizing the paragraph's main idea. However, topic sentences are also pithy statements that precede and polemicize an argument. In this expanded understanding, while topic sentences certainly provide the skeletal structure of a policy memo, they may also serve as the lead paragraph in a press release or the opening sound bite of a live television interview. They are the most fundamental building blocks of the various media we discuss in this text.

Strong topic sentences feature six essential attributes:

1) Summative
2) Clear
3) Succinct
4) Enticing
5) Argumentative
6) Transitional (in longer works)

First, strong topic sentences are summative. At their core, topic sentences act as a preview of what is to come. They signal the subject matter, scope, and direction of the paragraph or presentation that follows. Indeed, if strong topic sentences are crafted in written work, the reader should be able to read only the opening sentence of a paragraph and understand the entirety of the grander argument. To be sure, the reader will lose a sense of nuance and be deprived of examples and other important material. However, good topic sentences allow busy readers to skim your work without missing the main thrust of your analysis or idea.

The following are two examples of topic sentences that are summative of a general argument:

> Example 1a: There are three reasons that vitamins and nutritional supplements should be subject to more regulation.

> Example 1b: The Amazon rainforest is subject to threats arising from deforestation and climate change.

Notice how summative sentences simply lay out the content of an argument to follow. Rushed readers can move on to the next section or document with an overarching understanding. However, those with an interest in the justification and evidence of these arguments will read on for greater depth. Indeed, in the case of Example 1a, even a rushed reader will likely read the subsequent topic sentences pertaining to each of the three reasons for more regulation. Now consider a counterexample:

> Counterexample: "Until we have proof of severe health consequences, no action will be taken," the head of the Food and Drug Administration said last year.

This counterexample—a topic sentence that fails to be summative—uses a quotation without context. It can be tempting to begin paragraphs with rich quotations, but these rarely embody the principal argument you could otherwise craft yourself. Evidence should not be left to speak for itself. Other counterexamples may focus on a minor detail.

Second, strong topic sentences are clear. It is important to remember that these are introductory statements, so they need to be free of jargon, free from intimidation, free from ambiguity. Topic sentences are an invitation into an argument. This is especially important for complicated matters about which most people have limited understanding—whether science, technology, or even the tax code.[3] It is not

3. See Jamieson, K. (2015). Communicating the value and values of science. *Issues in Science and Technology*, *32*(1), 72–79. Retrieved from http://www.jstor.org.ezp-prod1.hul.harvard.edu/stable/24727008

incumbent on your readers or listeners to match your level of understanding; it is incumbent upon you as the author or speaker to clarify the complexity. Doing so will not suggest a simplistic understanding of the subject matter; rather, it demonstrates your mastery.

The following are two examples of topic sentences that clarify a general argument:

> Example 2a: The Food and Drug Administration (FDA) inadequately regulates vitamins and supplements.

> Example 2b: The deterioration of the Amazon rainforest is a fixable problem.

These two topic sentences relate to complicated subjects that most people know little about—the chemical composition of vitamins and nutritional supplements (along with their nutritional impact) and the ecology of a rainforest. However, the topics are presented in a clear and accessible manner. In the statements that follow these topic sentences, the author or speaker will no doubt introduce and incorporate a number of more complicated concepts, but the opening invites the reader or listener to learn more. It is worth noting that Example 2a spells out the FDA acronym in case readers are not familiar with the abbreviation. It is also worth noting how even basic jargon like "ecology" and "desertification" is absent from Example 2b.

> Counterexample: The DDI should more closely regulate herbal glycemic control remedies.

This counterexample shows the confusion that can result from unclear acronyms and jargon. Here, "DDI" refers to the

FDA's Division of Drug Information, while "glycemic control remedies" can be more easily stated as "treatments for diabetes." For good examples of accessible writing about complicated subjects, read the Associated Press' and Reuters' coverage of almost any topic but particularly science, health, and financial news—which can otherwise be quite complex and technical.

Third, strong topic sentences are succinct. Sometimes our written works and oral presentations are insufficiently clear and succinct because we feel pressure to demonstrate the full range of our expertise. Others feel pressure to encapsulate the full extent of their argument or the full depth of their analysis in the topic sentence. My father likes to joke, "It's hard to be succinct when I know so much." However, topic sentences are not about being comprehensive. Readers are not craving depth or range in a topic sentence. In fact, many readers are more likely to read on with less revealed; they are tempted by what may come. This is why questions often work well as topic sentences: they imply that an answer follows.

The following are two examples of topic sentences that communicate a general subject matter or argument in few words:

> Example 3a: Health supplements can harm.

> Example 3b: Who will protect the Amazon rainforest?

Example 3a demonstrates the force of short, punchy statements. The bluntness of this example shocks the reader into attention, while again communicating a clear argument that anticipates something to follow. Example 3b shows the power of a question. Questions stimulate curiosity, while also signaling the topic to be covered. And in this case, the question also suggests that the Amazon rainforest requires protection and that it is unclear who is committed to this cause. Reading these brief openings, were you concerned that the author lacked depth of knowledge? Surely not. We don't expect topic sentences to demonstrate the full range of expertise.

> Counterexample: Extraordinarily fertile and enormous, the Amazon rainforest is the largest rainforest in the world and critical to the Earth's atmosphere, yet its future is in question at the international level.

This counterexample—though grammatically correct—is hardly succinct. Although it includes far more information than Example 3b, it is less effective. The length of the sentence alone encourages the reader to skip ahead without absorbing the author's intended point. The reader is distracted by unnecessary detail such as "extraordinarily fertile and enormous." An adequate revision of this topic sentence would be, "Although critical to the Earth's atmosphere, the future of the Amazon rainforest is in question." As a convenient test of succinctness (and clarity), read your topic sentence aloud to yourself or another person. This often helps diagnose long-windedness and obscurity.

Fourth, strong topic sentences are enticing. Another reason why readers don't expect the author to reveal everything immediately is because we—as consumers of information, products, and services—are accustomed to being lured. Topic sentences can, therefore, also be understood as "advertisements." Such appeals should avoid deception while offering the most attractive prompts of what is to come. Just as a book title attempts to motivate readers to open the cover, topic sentences attempt to motivate the reader to consider reading the next sentence.

The following are two examples of topic sentences that are intended to attract readers and listeners to want more:

> Example 4a: The Food and Drug Administration has a blind spot.

> Example 4b: A loophole protects paper companies that destroy the rainforest.

As consumers of information, readers and listeners are most attracted to conflict and mystery. Conflict is ultimately about disagreement and opposition—controversy. This relates to the importance Saul Alinsky attributed to polarizing subject matters. Mystery engages the unknown or the counterintuitive, begging more information. Examples 4a and 4b engage both controversy and mystery. They solicit interest in a regulator's lapse and something that smacks of corruption or a conspiracy between government and industry. Beyond curiosity, they also implicitly tap into conventional concerns for justice. Consequently, readers are likely to be angered or intrigued by such statements; either way, they are likely to read on.

> Counterexample: Rainforests are important ecosystems.

This counterexample clarifies the subject matter and emphasizes its importance, without clarifying why it is important. Nevertheless, this is not a source of tension that will evoke emotion or attract readers to continue.

Fifth, strong topic sentences are argumentative. However, this attribute is only applicable to policy ideas that are subject to disagreement. In this very polarized political moment, it may be hard to imagine policy-relevant ideas that are not contentious. However, agencies like the Census Bureau, The World Bank, and the Bureau of Labor Statistics all produce reports and information that, while meriting broad publicity, are inherently objective and nonpartisan. However, in most cases, politics is about persuasion in the midst of contention. Indeed, parties and interests are seeking to profit from even the most benign government report from agencies like the Government Accountability Office. To be argumentative, ask yourself, "Are there people out there who would disagree?" If not or if the opposition is quite obscure, you are likely insufficiently argumentative.

The following are two examples of topic sentences that are argumentative:

> Example 5a: Producers of vitamins and nutritional supplements should be subject to the same oversight as the producers of other substances that advertise healing qualities.

> Example 5b: Local tribes are the world's most important partners in the struggle to protect the Amazon rainforest.

It will not be hard to find parties and interests that disagree with Examples 5a and 5b. Therefore, these statements are sufficiently argumentative. They serve as strong topic sentences because they take a side or assert a perspective.

> Counterexample: Different countries enforce different levels of oversight over vitamins and supplements.

This counterexample is well written and would be a good topic sentence for a body paragraph that seeks to offer evidence. But whereas a good topic sentence lays out an argument, this counterexample falls short by merely restating a mundane fact.

Sixth, and only when embedded in longer texts, strong topic sentences transition from one argument or subject matter to the next. In this way, they act as the hinges or flexpoints in memoranda, reports, and executive summaries in which the author wishes to pivot but not lose a connection with her or his main argument or subject matter. To do so, the author must find ways to link with what has already been written and link with what is to follow.

The following are two examples of topic sentences that transition from one argument or subject matter to the next:

> Example 6a: Without the resources of Big Pharma, vitamin producers have secured a sweetheart deal from the FDA.

> Example 6b: Despite this enhanced public interest, the Amazon Rainforest has diminished at the same pace.

In both Examples 6a and 6b, the first clause of the sentence clearly connects with a preceding statement. In Example 6a, we can infer that the author previously discussed the financial and lobbying power of large pharmaceutical companies or the relatively smaller resources of vitamin producers. In Example 6b, we can infer that the author previously discussed public interest in deforestation. In both cases, there is a second clause that—if separated from the first—could serve as an effective topic sentence alone. Both examples also advantageously use transition terms, “Despite” and “Without.”

Counterexample: In light of this, climate change policy should be rethought.

This counterexample attempts to transition, but it is not clear what conclusion from the preceding paragraph informs this paragraph: it is not clear what "this" refers to. Further, the second clause, while argumentative, is not descriptive enough to summarize the content of the paragraph to come. What type of policy? What aspects should be rethought? In what way? The second clause is too vague to stand on its own. Here, we see that transition terms cannot do all the work: the writer must also provide a summation of the analysis to come. This demonstrates how none of the topic sentence attributes are sufficient in isolation; they must be used together.

LESS IS MORE

The most difficult part of drafting strong topic sentences is attempting to achieve so much in very few words. Even for those of us who write for a living, our first attempts at topic sentences are far wordier and more complicated than necessary. Inside each of us, there is an inclination to be comprehensive—a fear of oversimplifying or omitting information. So instead, we write too much and communicate too little. Worse, when we overprovide, we confuse our readers and listeners. There is a paradox in trying to be comprehensive from the start: the more details we incorporate, the less clear we become. The more ways we justify our argument, the less convincing it sounds. The more angles we use to attract readers' attention, the fuzzier our argument appears and the less interest we generate.

In short, less is more. This law of parsimony is often called "Ockham's razor"—a principle attributed to William of Ockham in the 14th century that guided the development of scientific theories. This principle suggests that simpler arguments are preferable to more complex theses because they are more testable. And while it does not contend that simpler arguments are more likely to be valid, it does imply they are more convincing because every assumption we add to a contention weakens its universality (and feasibility) in application. Readers and listeners naturally grow increasingly skeptical with every condition you place on the credibility of your ideas.

A central challenge is to search your findings, your analysis, or your campaign for a single theme around which you may organize your outreach. This is true for all media we discuss in this text. Singularity helps you satisfy the first four criteria we covered in the previous section on topic sentences. First, single ideas lend themselves to the production of a summative statement, which necessarily omits details. Second, single ideas improve clarity by filtering out competing or supplementary ideas, which may otherwise confuse. Third, single ideas permit the greatest degree of succinctness. And fourth, single ideas are not only more attractive and convincing, according to Ockham's razor, but also more memorable and transferable. In short, the goal is to simplify without being simplistic.

Identifying singular themes or arguments requires a mix of acumen and brutality. True expertise renders people the clarity of focus to discern what is genuinely new or advanced. When we are truly capable of grasping the state of our respective fields, we are able to communicate the ideas that will be the most interesting or impactful. However, experts are often far less able to be brutal in editing ideas down to their core. Due to a mix of self-absorption and myopia, we have spent too much time developing our memo, platform, or book to discard 99 percent of its content. We are too close to it to determine what is the most attractive element. In such cases—and in the absence of an editor or a publicity team—it is helpful to have friends or colleagues review your work to verify that what you think is broadly compelling actually is that compelling. To be truly brutal, distance can be quite helpful.

The remainder of this book discusses the most effective ways to communicate your policy ideas in multiple media. In this way, you may advance beyond the brevity of the tweet and topic sentences, without losing their main properties. Given the challenges of condensing complicated ideas, we will work from the lengthiest media to those most limited by space and time. We will also move from written media forms to those that are orally and electronically delivered.

2

THE EXECUTIVE SUMMARY

PRINCIPLES

Reaching Policymakers and Wonks

Imagine that your friend asked you, "What did you do last weekend?" How would you respond? You would not describe every weekend activity to your friend, but you would certainly attempt to present an account that included the highlights and probably some of the most interesting stories. (You don't want to seem like you have no social life!)

Imagine that your boss asked you, "What did I miss at the meeting you attended?" How would you respond here? You would "bring her up to speed." In most cases, this would not entail telling your boss about your coworker falling asleep during the boring presentation the office has heard dozens of times. Rather, you would ensure that you share any information your boss may not already know but would be expected to know.

Every day, we informally deliver executive summaries to our family, friends, and colleagues when we condense our experiences or ideas clearly and concisely. As part of an attempt to communicate policy ideas, executive summaries are no different. You want to present the most important components of a far longer study, analysis, or platform in a fraction of the space.

In this way, the executive summary is akin to the chef who boils down wine or vinegar to burn off the water content and concentrate its essential flavors—in short, a reduction. Executive summaries boil down the content of a longer piece of work to distill its most essential ideas, findings, and conclusions. Like a reduction sauce, the substance of the original material necessarily changes: the wine reduction is no longer solely cabernet; however, the flavor of the wine, along with other components, endures.

Authors face the difficulty of concentrating a diffuse subject into a compact discussion. As we discussed in Chapter 1, this is because many authors find themselves quite wed to the original productions or outputs. Invested in the content of the full work (and the effort to produce it), authors often overvalue the details of the original to the detriment of communicating the work's essential thrust. Other authors are simply proud of this rigor or nuance and don't want it to be lost on busy readers who never turn past the summary. It is important to understand that such detail is not extraneous; it is just not required to understand the report's contribution.

As a rule of thumb, executive summaries should not comprise more than 10 percent of the full-length memo or report, and this should not exceed more than ten pages, even for the longest documents. In Washington, DC, the Heritage Foundation is credited with the development of a "limousine memo." The idea behind the limousine memo is that it should be possible to read the memo in the time it takes a member of Congress to travel in a limousine from the White House to the Capitol, that is, roughly ten minutes.

Structure

Executive summaries exist thanks to the assumption that busy people will not read an entire, full-length report. (Some think that the production of executive summaries ensures that this assumption is true, that an executive summary reduces the psychological incentive to read the full memo.) In preparing one, your goal is to provide the most compelling overview possible such that the reader will be motivated to read on or will simply be persuaded by the summary alone. In many ways, the executive summary *is* your memo.

Reading an executive summary is like reading a string of topic sentences. Indeed, if your topic sentences transition well enough, they could even comprise much of your executive summary. Removing the paragraphs that present and discuss examples, the following is a compilation of all of the topic sentences from Chapter 1:

> *Written text is at the core of almost all products in society. Why would public policy and policy campaigns be any different? The problem with public policy materials—analyses, platforms, and bills—is that these foundational texts are written to be well referenced, rigorous, and possibly legally binding; they are not written to be broadly read.*
>
> *Public policy ideas, therefore, require authors and advocates to promote their ideas in the public sphere. There are three key components to these media conversions, the first of which is the material. Second, the text is as much about the messenger as it is about the message. Third, you must select the appropriate medium and venue for your message. For this reason, the more media in which you can fluently communicate your message, the more effective you will be.*

> *Topic sentences are the backbone of all written work and each of these media. Strong topic sentences feature six essential attributes. First, strong topic sentences are summative. Second, strong topic sentences are clear. Third, strong topic sentences are succinct. Fourth, strong topic sentences are enticing. Fifth, strong topic sentences are argumentative. Sixth, and only when embedded in longer texts, strong topic sentences transition from one argument or subject matter to the next. The most difficult part of drafting strong topic sentences is attempting to achieve so much in very few words. In short, less is more. A central challenge is to search your findings, your analysis, or your campaign for a single theme around which you may organize your outreach. Identifying singular themes or arguments requires a mix of acumen and brutality. The remainder of this book discusses the most effective ways to communicate your policy ideas in multiple media.*

This example acts to demonstrate the way that topic sentences form the skeletal structure that may, on its own, constitute a summary. While it is not advisable to exclusively use them to produce a formal executive summary, the executive summary of Chapter 1 does the job. It consists of 288 words, about 8 percent of the chapter's word count. And from this executive summary, the casual reader is able to grasp the chapter's primary points. However, it is ultimately an inadequate substitute for actually reading Chapter 1 in full. Were you to only read the executive summary, you would not grasp the importance of polarization, you would not understand references to Ockham's razor, and you may not know how to apply the six attributes of topic sentences. Similarly, were I to only draft the executive summary and not include elaborations of my broader claims, it would not be particularly worthy of publication. Still, for someone considering whether to read Chapter 1 or whether to assign Chapter 1, the summary would be helpful. Even readers who plan to read the entire memo usually read the executive summary in order to clarify the main points or know where to focus their attention.

In light of people's reliance on executive summaries, these summaries present authors with an important opportunity to sharpen the focus of their analysis. There are a number of techniques you may employ to do this.

START WITH A SHORT, PUNCHY TITLE AND A SHORT, PUNCHY OPENING THAT CAPTURES YOUR MEMO'S PRINCIPAL ARGUMENT

This is the topic sentence for your entire memo. When the memo or its authors are interested stakeholders, the principal argument should come first. Indeed, even when the work is objective, it is reasonable to lead with your principal finding and describe its credibility and context shortly thereafter. Recent research suggests that science journals which publish papers with shorter titles receive more citations per paper.[1]

PROVIDE A REFERENCE TO THE CONTEXT OF THE WORK ITSELF

Who undertook the work? What research did it entail? What scoping conditions were necessary? When subjects are

1. Letchford, A., Moat, H. S., & Preis, T. (2015). The advantage of short paper titles. *Royal Society Open Science*, *2*, 150266. Retrieved from http://dx.doi.org/10.1098/rsos.150266; Jamali, H. R., & Nikzad, M. (2011). Article title type and its relation with the number of downloads and citations. *Scientometrics*, *88*(2), 653–661.

politically charged, it is especially important to describe the extent to which your work is objective—such as in cases when you are providing a nonpartisan evaluation, a commissioned report, an academic study, a formal audit, or an official investigation. In these cases, it is advisable to lead with this context by describing the rigor of the study's methods or design to establish your credibility. Part of the appeal of nonpartisan research is the rigorous methodological foundations. If you've taken the steps to ensure that your work minimizes bias, reap the benefits of sharing that. Even when the work is not objective or not executed by a dispassionate party, it is important to clarify your methods up front. In these cases, though, it is advisable to lead not with the context but rather with your most important conclusion.

UNDERSCORE THE KEY COMPONENTS OF YOUR PRINCIPAL IDEA

What are the subfindings and subarguments that ground the broader conclusion? These are effectively the topic sentences from each of the sectional components of broader reports. Each component should clearly link to the principal idea and follow a straightforward logic. This is your opportunity to show how various pieces of the analysis fit together.

CITE PAGE NUMBERS OR STRUCTURE FOR EASY NAVIGATION TO CONTENT

Because each statement links directly to a section of the full memo you produce, you can place the page number that corresponds with the elaborated section in parentheses. This facilitates the engagement of busy readers who are initially inclined to only read the executive summary but become interested in one component of your work and want to read further content. For readers who plan to engage with the text as a whole, providing page numbers in the executive summary helps them focus their consumption of your material. The summary can be structured in a way that directly outlines the rest of the report or analysis. For example, headings in the summary should correspond to chapter or section titles. The executive summary will then double as an annotated table of contents.

PUNCTUATE THE TEXT WITH EMPHASIS

Multiple long paragraphs can intimidate or bore busy readers. To create a sense of currency, use active-voice formulations rather than passive-voice formulations. Find ways to interrupt the monotony of the text to channel their attention. A list is a useful way to consolidate key ideas into a clear, memorable format. Bullet points, timelines, and sequential steps work in a similar way. You may also wish to—selectively—use **bold** or *italicized* text, or subheadings. It is important to use these techniques selectively because overuse of font manipulation will lead to marginally lower impact and undermine the sophistication of your work.

PRACTITIONERS

Alexandra Sicotte-Levesque *is the head of community engagement at the International Federation of Red Cross and Red Crescent Societies. Previously, she served as the coordinator for community engagement in the Office for the Coordination of Humanitarian Affairs at the UN. Before her career with global governance institutions, Sicotte-Levesque worked as a* *radio producer for UN radio in Sudan (Radio Miraya) and the country director for the BBC World Service Trust in Sudan. In 2002, she cofounded Journalists for Human Rights, for which she was awarded a Meritorious Service Medal (Canada) by the Canadian governor-general. She has also directed two award-winning films,* When Silence Is Golden, *about the impact of Canadian gold mining activities on a small town in western Ghana, and* The Longest Kiss, *which examines Sudanese youth ahead of the country's split.* ***Ralph Mamiya*** *is an independent consultant who previously led the Protection of Civilians Team in the UN Department of Peacekeeping Operations and Department of Field Support. He has spent more than ten years working on peacekeeping and protection issues, including tours with UN missions in Sudan and South Sudan. He has published articles on international law and international relations, including the* Oxford Handbook on the Use of Force in International Law *(2015), and is a coeditor of the volume* Protection of Civilians *(2016, Oxford University Press). I asked Ms. Sicotte-Levesque and Mr. Mamiya (who are married) to share their collective advice about preparing executive summaries. Here are their thoughts:*

> Let us be honest: the executive summary of a policy report or research study will most often be the only part of the document that policymakers will read. Taking the time to read several 20- or 50-page reports may be a luxury for your audience, whether they are government officials or United Nations staff. The need to read such a report must compete with the urgency of many other tasks such as attending meetings, drafting memos, and, well, attending more meetings. Knowing how to write a good executive summary is, therefore, an important skill to have if you want your work to have an impact. And

so one of the most important skills in professional writing is learning to write for people who have little time to spend on each document.

Here are four characteristics of a good executive summary:

First, it should read as a stand-alone document. While it summarizes a larger piece of research or study, you shouldn't have to read through the main document to discover the main points. Remember, even though your recommendations may be aimed at a government, you may want journalists to use your report or study to cover the issue. This can maximize the impact of your study on the public, and, again, journalists will likely refer first to your executive summary. Your writing should, therefore, be as compelling as possible.

Second, unlike an abstract of an academic study, an executive summary should outline the key policy recommendations and the key data that support those recommendations. Data, when available, can make a strong point. If you have new and unique data in your report, make sure you include these data in your executive summary.

Third, your writing should be tailored to your readership. For instance, the content of a report on human rights violations in South Sudan may contain similar facts whether it is drafted by the United Nations High Commissioner for Human Rights or by the nonprofit organization Human Rights Watch. The executive summaries, however, may be very different. The UN report may be addressed to the Human Rights Council, which is composed of many different nations, some of which have questionable human rights records themselves; such a summary may be relatively clinical in tone. For an advocacy organization such as Human Rights Watch, however, the executive summary may be advocating for change in US or UN policy, independent of political sensitivities.

Fourth, the writing should be clear, simple, and concise. Avoid jargon (unless you define it) and go straight to the point as quickly as possible. It's okay to use bullet points to highlight recommendations. Clarity of message takes precedence over background information and style. Similarly, off-putting stylistic choices, such as repetition of important words or phrases, may be necessary to ensure that the message is conveyed clearly and quickly.

Knowing how to summarize a long document is a valuable skill. You know you have it when you are able to read a lengthy document, take notes along the way, and condense the key points that emanate from the report. These are the same skills used in drafting talking points, briefing notes, and similar documents common throughout modern organizations. As with many types of writing, perhaps the best way to develop a skill in drafting executive summaries is practice. Think about how you might describe the contents of a long report to a friend over a drink. Read as many executive summaries as possible to see what works and what doesn't and then identify their strengths. Then find someone close to you who is willing to read your executive summary and give you feedback. This person doesn't have to be an expert in your field, but rather someone who is generally informed and an avid reader, who can tell you if they are understanding your ideas clearly, if they are bored, or if they can summarize your summary accurately. In many cases, you will likely receive feedback from your boss, client, or principal, too.

In many organizations, including the UN and the US government, staff at every level use executive summaries to prepare their supervisors. They then use this information to prepare *their* supervisors, and so on up to the level at which decisions are made. Sometimes these summaries reach the very highest level, such as the secretary-general or the president of a country. In this chain, when it works properly, vast amounts of information are condensed and synthesized, and important decisions follow.

PARAGON

At the conclusion of each chapter, I provide a full, unedited example of the communications medium I discuss. Here, I offer but one of the many executive summaries produced each year by the Congressional Budget Office (CBO), a nonpartisan government office that produces independent, impartial analyses of budgetary and economic issues to support the US congressional budget process. The following is the executive summary of a 37-page report on the American Health Care Act, a Republican-proposed bill, backed by the Trump administration, that would have repealed the Affordable Care Act, also known as "Obamacare." Few will actually read every page and appreciate all the methodological detail the report contains. However, the report begins with an introduction that offers an overview of its findings. Bold headings and consistent paragraph structure make the content easy to navigate or skim. Punchy prose clarifies the findings. This CBO report was among the most widely read reports in the CBO's history and ultimately was a principal reason for the bill's failure to pass the House of Representatives, despite a large Republican majority.

CONGRESSIONAL BUDGET OFFICE
COST ESTIMATE

May 24, 2017

H.R. 1628
American Health Care Act of 2017

As passed by the House of Representatives on May 4, 2017

SUMMARY

American Health Care Act
March 13, 2017

CBO and JCT [Joint Committee on Taxation] estimate that enacting the American Health Care Act would reduce federal deficits by $337 billion over the coming decade and increase the number of people who are uninsured by 24 million in 2026 relative to current law.

The Concurrent Resolution on the Budget for Fiscal Year 2017 directed the House Committees on Ways and Means and Energy and Commerce to develop legislation to reduce the deficit. The Congressional Budget Office and the staff of the Joint Committee on Taxation (JCT) have produced an estimate of the budgetary effects of the American Health Care Act, which combines the pieces of legislation approved by the two committees pursuant to that resolution. In consultation with the budget committees, CBO used its March 2016 baseline with adjustments for subsequently enacted legislation, which underlies the resolution, as the benchmark to measure the cost of the legislation.

Effects on the Federal Budget

CBO and JCT estimate that enacting the legislation would reduce federal deficits by $337 billion over the 2017–2026 period. That total consists of $323 billion in on-budget savings and $13 billion in off-budget savings. Outlays would be reduced by $1.2 trillion over the period, and revenues would be reduced by $0.9 trillion.

The largest savings would come from reductions in outlays for Medicaid and from the elimination of the Affordable Care Act's (ACA's) subsidies for nongroup health insurance. The largest costs would come from repealing many of the changes the ACA made to the Internal Revenue Code—including an increase in the Hospital Insurance payroll tax rate for high-income taxpayers, a surtax on those taxpayers' net investment income and annual fees imposed on health insurers—and from the establishment of a new tax credit for health insurance.

Pay-as-you-go procedures apply because enacting the legislation would affect direct spending and revenues. CBO and JCT estimate that enacting the legislation would not increase net direct spending or on-budget deficits by more than $5 billion in any of the four consecutive ten-year periods beginning in 2027.

Effects on Health Insurance Coverage

To estimate the budgetary effects, CBO and JCT projected how the legislation would change the number of people who obtain federally subsidized health insurance through Medicaid, the nongroup market, and the employment-based market, as well as many other factors.

CBO and JCT estimate that, in 2018, 14 million more people would be uninsured under the legislation than under current law. Most of that increase would stem from repealing the penalties associated with the individual mandate. Some of those people would choose not to have insurance because they chose to be covered by insurance under current law only to avoid paying the penalties, and some people would forgo insurance in response to higher premiums.

Later, following additional changes to subsidies for insurance purchased in the nongroup market and to the Medicaid program, the increase in the number of uninsured people relative to the number under current law would rise to 21 million in 2020 and then to 24 million in 2026. The reductions in insurance coverage between 2018 and 2026 would stem in large part from changes in Medicaid enrollment—because some states would discontinue their expansion of eligibility, some states that would have expanded eligibility in the future would choose not to do so and per-enrollee spending in the program would be capped. In 2026, an estimated 52 million people would be uninsured, compared with 28 million who would lack insurance that year under current law.

Stability of the Health Insurance Market

Decisions about offering and purchasing health insurance depend on the stability of the health insurance market—that is, on having insurers participating in most areas of the country and on the likelihood of premiums' not rising in an unsustainable spiral. The market for insurance purchased individually (that is, nongroup coverage) would be unstable, for example, if the people who wanted to buy coverage at any offered price would have average health care expenditures so high that offering the insurance would be unprofitable. In CBO and JCT's assessment, however, the nongroup market would probably be stable in most areas under either current law or the legislation.

Under current law, most subsidized enrollees purchasing health insurance coverage in the nongroup market are largely insulated from increases in premiums because their out-of-pocket payments for premiums are based on a percentage of their income; the government pays the difference. The subsidies to purchase coverage combined with the penalties paid by uninsured people stemming from the individual mandate are anticipated to cause sufficient demand for insurance by people with low health care expenditures for the market to be stable.

Under the legislation, in the agencies' view, key factors bringing about market stability include subsidies to purchase insurance, which would maintain sufficient demand for insurance by people with low health care expenditures, and grants to states from the Patient and State Stability Fund, which would reduce the costs to insurers of people with high health care expenditures. Even though the new tax credits would be structured differently from the current subsidies and would generally be less generous for those receiving subsidies under current law, the other changes would, in the agencies' view, lower average premiums enough to attract a sufficient number of relatively healthy people to stabilize the market.

Effects on Premiums

The legislation would tend to increase average premiums in the nongroup market prior to 2020 and lower average premiums thereafter, relative to projections under current law. In 2018 and 2019, according to CBO and JCT's estimates, average premiums for single policyholders in the nongroup market would be 15 percent to 20 percent higher than under current law, mainly because the individual mandate penalties would be eliminated, inducing fewer comparatively healthy people to sign up.

Starting in 2020, the increase in average premiums from repealing the individual mandate penalties would be more than offset by the combination of several factors that would decrease those premiums: grants to states from the Patient and State Stability Fund (which CBO and JCT expect to largely be used by states to limit the costs to insurers of enrollees with very high claims); the elimination of the requirement for insurers to offer plans covering certain percentages of the cost of covered benefits; and a younger mix of enrollees. By 2026, average premiums for single policyholders in the nongroup market under the legislation would be roughly 10 percent lower than under current law, CBO and JCT estimate.

Although average premiums would increase prior to 2020 and decrease starting in 2020, CBO and JCT estimate that changes in premiums relative to those under current law would differ significantly for people of different ages because of a change in age-rating rules. Under the legislation, insurers would be allowed to generally charge five times more for older enrollees than younger ones rather than three times more as under current law, substantially reducing premiums for young adults and substantially raising premiums for older people.

THE PRESS RELEASE

PRINCIPLES

Reaching Journalists

Press releases are the raw material of journalism. Like textiles in the fashion industry, they are ultimately converted into more elaborate and amalgamated products that make the original material sometimes unrecognizable. However, they provide the initial basis for production. The language of even the best press releases is rarely fully incorporated into journalistic articles or commentary. From their earliest assignments, journalists are trained to be skeptical of information provided by the subject they seek to investigate, to not accept it at face value. There is always more detail or background or a way to corroborate the information provided. There is often a local context to apply. There is always another perspective to consider—dispassionate or opposing parties who will offer juicier, more candid statements than those provided by the newsmaker.

For journalists to print a press release, therefore, is a capitulation to press secretaries and publicists who seek to control the flow of information. What is the use of journalism in societies that protect the freedom of speech if we allow entities of authority to word the news in the manner they desire? It is worth noting that press releases can also have different intentions. Some newsmakers want to cover up or distract from unflattering news. Other newsmakers procedurally release information as a formality. In light of this book's focus on communicating policy ideas, my discussion is specific to press releases that seek to attract as much attention as possible—to contribute to, or even define, a public debate.

Consequently, the writers of press releases aim not to be published themselves but rather to provide a basis for further reporting—a glimpse of the news article your release may ultimately become. They introduce the journalist and public to your primary arguments, the relevant stakeholders, and the background they need to know before embarking on further reporting. Consequently, unlike journalists' reporting, press releases do not typically feature the flair or pizzazz typical of the mainstream media. That is generally left to journalists to create. Press releases aim to simply inform effectively and persuasively.

Despite the fact that newsmakers know that the verbatim content of press releases may not see the light of day, they are constantly seeking ways to influence what is ultimately published. Often, former journalists themselves, press secretaries, and publicists know that journalists are always very busy and pressured by deadlines. This is even truer now that about 75 percent of readers peruse news sources on the internet.[1] Whereas reporters used to have the whole day to

1. Newman, N., Fletcher, R., Levy, D., & Nielsen R. (2016). *Reuters Institute digital news report 2016*. Oxford, UK: Reuters Institute for the Study of Journalism.

develop their stories before their publication went to the printing press, journalists in the digital era are incentivized to publish their stories online as soon as possible. As a result of shifting and pressing deadlines and despite their inherent skepticism about officially provided information, hurried journalists are likely to rely on this information in the absence of other sources or in the absence of time to cultivate other sources. Indeed, competition among journalists to "scoop" the competition is so tight now that many publications will initially publish the basic content of press releases online and modify it throughout the day.

Structure

With the prospect of incorporation into news articles, press releases are best written with the structure and components of a news article. And, like news articles, speed is often essential. Unless your organization owns the news—such as when the White House announces an executive order or judicial appointment—you are competing with other organizations to influence the direction of the coverage. However, press releases also feature structural and stylistic components that reflect the fact that they are, ultimately, different from actual news articles.

DATELINE

The dateline is the brief piece of text you are accustomed to reading at the beginning of news articles that describes the location and time that the article was filed. This is largely ornamental, but it gives the press release the veneer of a news article. Note that press releases usually do not have a byline; in other words, they do not list the author. This is because the release is sharing information attributable to an organization or office rather than to an individual. (However, it is important that the press release lists a contact person. See the section below, "Logistics.")

INVERTED PYRAMID

The inverted pyramid is a classic journalism metaphor that represents the manner in which information should be provided in a work of reporting. Thinking of pieces of information schematically, whereby the most important details are given the most weight, the inverted pyramid represents the placement of the weightiest elements at the top of the article, followed sequentially by those of incrementally less significance. There are two primary criteria for determining which information is more important for placement purposes. The first criterion is simply a matter that will generate the most interest from the greatest number of people in your target readership. This may be a powerful anecdote or sensational statement. Behavioral science research shows that people connect more closely with (and better remember) a story—character-driven portraits of a person or movement with emotional content to which people can relate.[2]

The desire to attract must be balanced by a concern for the second criterion, which asks what information the reader will demand.[3] This is often more practical or descriptive

2. Tversky, A., Kahneman, D., & Hoffman, Martin L. (1983). Extensional versus intuitive reasoning: The conjunction fallacy in probability judgment. *Psychological Review*, *90*(4), 293–315.

3. E.g., Sehgal, K. (2016). How to write email with military precision. *Harvard Business Review*, November 22. Retrieved from https://hbr.org/2016/11/how-to-write-email-with-military-precision

aspects of the policy issues (e.g., timing, official records, availability, eligibility criteria, how-to). As a result, you will tend to see press releases swing back and forth, splicing practical information in between juicy quotes. Sometimes these criteria align: that which is the most interesting can also be practical.

THE LEAD

Naturally, the inverted pyramid means that you begin with the most important, most novel piece of information that will interest or affect the largest population of readers. This opening is called the "lead" (or alternatively, the "lede"). The lead is a topic sentence, like any other. However, this topic sentence is under a great deal of pressure to attract interest in the story. In a highly competitive public sphere, filled with other events and ideas, ensure that you draft the lead to generate the greatest attention. However, as this lead will be written in a journalistic manner, this topic sentence must also cover the "who," "what," "when," and "where" of the event. An example:

> A coalition of small businesses and anti-poverty organizations today condemned the White House plan to shield American workers from the effects of the coronavirus pandemic, calling the proposal "little more than a life vest."

QUOTATIONS

Like any news article, press releases contain quotations from relevant people involved in the announcement, event, or issue. These quotations are often called "canned" because they are carefully crafted and packaged by the press release authors to support the perspective they seek to communicate.

While you must receive permission from the person to whom each quotation will be attributed, you have the luxury of editing them to suit the press release content and its goals. Canned quotes are often not especially colorful, but they can present an opportunity to invigorate an otherwise dry topic, humanize an abstract subject matter, or polemicize a seemingly uncontroversial issue. This is the space for analogy, metaphor, and rhetoric amid otherwise journalistic prose.

HYPERLINKS, TWEETS, AND VIDEO

Modern press releases no longer need to passively mention people, documents, and external support for their ideas. You may embed hyperlinks that connect to materials and profiles you reference. You may insert supportive tweets from key players. These can be lieu of, or in addition to, canned quotes. Furthermore, you may embed video. All of this helps steer journalists to the supporting content that you want to appear in any coverage of your ideas or campaign. And it makes the press release more engaging for the nonjournalistic public should you choose to target a broader audience.

HISTORY AND BACKGROUND

Press releases are also an opportunity to clarify the history or timeline of an issue in a manner that most suits your perspective. Because journalists often rely on press releases to orient themselves to unfamiliar issues, the back end of a press release is an opportunity to bring readers up to date about recent or related events. Like every piece of material they produce, press officers regularly "spin" these materials to advance their agenda. While you may be tempted to do the same (and true objectivity is impossible), placing too much spin undermines your credibility and the credibility of the other materials you produce.

FACT SHEETS

Fact sheets are now also used as, or as part of, press releases to brief members of the news media who may choose to write or speak about a controversial subject. When fact sheets are produced by non-objective organizations, such as campaigns, elected officials, cabinet offices, think tanks, or civil society organizations, such evidence is typically tilted to favor an espoused position. However, for independent researchers from objective government agencies (such as the Inspector General's office, the Government Accountability Office, the Federal Election Commission, the Food and Drug Administration, or a statistics office like the Bureau of Labor Statistics or the US Census) or independent research universities, these fact sheets will usually avoid. Similarly, the source may make personnel available for interviews and offer similar logistical details.

LOGISTICS

Because press releases are instruments of publicity rather than actual journalism, they serve a practical purpose and must provide logistical information to journalists. This information includes the following:

1) Embargo period: An embargo period is a period of time when the publication of certain information or materials is not permitted. The press release should either say "For immediate release" or, if there is an embargo period, when the information can be released. If you would like to impose an

embargo period, simply write, "Embargo until [time and date]." Despite the pressure to publish information, journalists respect embargo periods not only as a norm to maintain a good reputation with their counterparts and colleagues but also in the interest of incentivizing press officials to share information in advance of its official release in the future.

2) A schedule of press conferences or media availability.
3) A contact person for journalists to contact with queries. This should include links to email, Facebook, Twitter, and any other social media used.

PRACTITIONER

Kathy Gest *is the president of the National Press Foundation, and a retired public affairs and communications strategist. (She is also my fourth cousin by marriage.) She served eight years as public affairs director for the National Democratic Institute, a nongovernmental organization specializing in democracy building. Previously, she cochaired the international practice at Powell Tate | Weber Shandwick, advising foreign governments, embassies, organizations, and corporations seeking to achieve public policy goals in the United States and abroad. She spent ten years as the press secretary to US Senator William Cohen of Maine, serving as his chief spokesperson and communications strategist and supporting his work as the lead Republican on the Governmental Affairs Oversight Subcommittee, Chair of the Special Committee on Aging, and Member of the Armed Services Committee. She also was a journalist for 16 years, most recently at* Congressional Quarterly, *where she held numerous reporting and editing posts, including managing editor.*

She was also an adjunct professor at Johns Hopkins University. I asked her to share her advice about preparing press releases. Here are her thoughts:

Whirlwind changes have taken place in recent years in the way information is delivered. But one thing that has not changed is the need for that information to be clear, concise, factual, and interesting if it is to have an impact.

All of those attributes can be found in a good press release, a century-old technique for conveying information. While distribution methods have evolved—from mail to fax to email to text messaging—there is no better way to get your message across on your own terms. I'm frequently asked, "How can I get better news coverage?" The answer is, you have to have something interesting to say, and you have to present it in a way that will make people want to read it—because it's unusual, new, not too long, easily understood, and well written. Having an enticing picture or video to go with it will help.

Concentrate on why you're writing the release. Are you making an announcement, commenting on an action, explaining what's happening at an event, or positioning for the future? All are legitimate reasons for a public statement. Defining the reason often defines the audience and how the release is written. Is the audience a general one that knows little or nothing about the subject, or are you aiming at experts in the field? The language in each case likely will be different.

News organizations are more likely to pick up your information if it's factual, straightforward, uses compelling language and interesting facts, and is even-handed, just like something that would appear in a well-written newspaper. But that doesn't mean it can't have a point of view.

Some years ago, I was involved in publicizing a report by the then General Accounting Office saying that Russian participation in the International Space Station would cost the United States a lot of money. In the press release announcing the findings, the senator who commissioned the report could have said merely that Russian involvement was too expensive. Instead he called the space station "a financial black hole," a quote that conjured up an image and was picked up widely by the news media. The first paragraph of that press release gave just the facts about what the report said. The quote told readers what the senator wanted them to think about those facts. The headline, which used the "black hole" line, was intended to get the attention of the news media and entice them to keep reading.

The political commentator Walter Lippmann wrote eloquently about how the pictures inside people's heads form their public opinions. A good writer will use imaginative, colorful language to create mental pictures that will influence how people think. Using well-chosen words in your press release, and avoiding jargon and buzz words, will help persuade readers to your point of view.

One way to do this is to break down big numbers and arcane concepts into human terms with good quotes and understandable facts. A Senate investigation into Medicare and Medicaid showed that fraud and abuse had cost taxpayers $418 billion over five years. It's a mind-boggling number beyond the experience of most people. The press release on the investigation broke it down, observing that the government was losing $275 million a day, or $11.5 million every hour. The senator who undertook the investigation, William Cohen of Maine, said in the press release, "It is shockingly simple to defraud the Federal Government."

Remarkable details can also increase interest. A number of years ago, another Senate investigation looked into inefficiencies in how the government was buying computers. It cited many examples of waste, but one in particular caught the attention of journalists. It revealed that the Federal Aviation Administration was buying vacuum tubes in Poland and going to Radio Shack stores to look for spare parts to keep its antiquated air traffic control tower computers running. For one of the network correspondents who covered the story, a computer exhibit at the Smithsonian Institution served as a backdrop. It was the only other place where one of the outdated computers could be found.

The most difficult part of press release writing is getting started. You must have in hand all the facts about your topic. Accuracy is the most important attribute of any release. You also need buy-in from all the parties involved—the people who created the information you're publicizing, anyone who will be mentioned in the release, and anyone who needs to give approval before the information can be made public. In addition, you need to anticipate what critics and opponents might say about what you're writing and have answers ready. You could include something in the release that will head off their arguments, but you have to be careful not to highlight negatives that might not be noticed otherwise.

While most press releases are written to prompt media coverage, there are other good reasons for doing them. One is just to get a statement on the record. An organization might put a release on its website, Facebook page, or Twitter feed (in abbreviated form) simply to ensure that its position is clear to anyone who comes looking for it. A related reason is to make clear to or impress allied groups or partners that their positions are in sync with yours. And still another, often used by organizations, corporations, and campaigns, is to reassure internal audiences that people at the top are doing the right thing.

Finally, before you send out or post anything, make sure there are no mistakes—no misspelled names or words, no factual errors, no grammatical problems, and no confusing language. You don't want anything you've written to be subject to misinterpretation. Nothing is worse than having to issue a retraction or correction. It undermines your credibility and immediately ensures that your message will be taken less seriously.

Press release writing can be a creative and rewarding experience, and even topics that might seem boring at first glance can be brought to life with imaginative language and good examples. Put some time into resourceful thinking at the beginning of the process, and you should be happy with the result.

PARAGON

The National Aeronautics and Space Administration (NASA) undertakes some of the most pioneering research and exploration in the world. NASA operates in the realm of cutting-edge astrophysics and theoretical physics to which few of us can relate or understand. And yet their work can be immensely important to our daily lives. For example, earlier breakthroughs have paved the way for the global communication network upon which we all depend. To maintain its operating budget and taxpayer support, NASA must find ways to make its findings and work relevant to the average person—the task of its public relations teams. Recently, NASA-backed scientists have used extraordinarily powerful telescopes to identify over a thousand planets in galaxies hundreds and thousands of light-years away. We know very little about these bodies of gas, rock, and metal; and they are given anonymous names like Kepler 452-a and Kepler 452-b. However, this work is brought to life by the intrigue associated with other worlds that may be like Earth and its inhabitants. Referring to one of them as an older "cousin to Earth" and an "Earth 2.0," this press release by Felicia Chou and Michele Johnson made international news.

(a)

(b)

July 23, 2015—Washington, DC

NASA's Kepler Mission Discovers Bigger, Older Cousin to Earth

NASA's Kepler mission has confirmed the first near-Earth-size planet in the "habitable zone" around a sun-like star. This discovery and the introduction of 11 other new small habitable zone candidate planets mark another milestone in the journey to finding another "Earth."

The newly discovered Kepler-452b is the smallest planet to date discovered orbiting in the habitable zone—the area around a star where liquid water could pool on the surface of an orbiting planet—of a G2-type star, like our sun. The confirmation of Kepler-452b brings the total number of confirmed planets to 1,030.

"On the 20th anniversary year of the discovery that proved other suns host planets, the Kepler exoplanet explorer has discovered a planet and star which most closely resemble the Earth and our Sun," said John Grunsfeld, associate administrator of NASA's Science Mission Directorate at the agency's headquarters in Washington. "This exciting result brings us one step closer to finding an Earth 2.0."

Kepler-452b is 60 percent larger in diameter than Earth and is considered a super-Earth-size planet. While its mass and composition are not yet determined, previous research suggests that planets the size of Kepler-452b have a good chance of being rocky.

While Kepler-452b is larger than Earth, its 385-day orbit is only 5 percent longer. The planet is 5 percent farther from its parent star Kepler-452 than Earth is from the Sun. Kepler-452 is 6 billion years old, 1.5 billion years older than our sun, has the same temperature, and is 20 percent brighter and has a diameter 10 percent larger.

"We can think of Kepler-452b as an older, bigger cousin to Earth, providing an opportunity to understand and reflect upon Earth's evolving environment," said Jon Jenkins, Kepler data analysis lead at NASA's Ames Research Center in Moffett Field, California, who led the team that discovered Kepler-452b. "It's awe-inspiring to consider that this planet has spent 6 billion years in the habitable zone of its star; longer than Earth. That's substantial opportunity for life to arise, should all the necessary ingredients and conditions for life exist on this planet."

To help confirm the finding and better determine the properties of the Kepler-452 system, the team conducted ground-based observations at the University of Texas at Austin's McDonald Observatory, the Fred Lawrence Whipple Observatory on Mt. Hopkins, Arizona, and the W. M. Keck Observatory atop Mauna Kea in Hawaii. These measurements were key for the researchers to confirm the planetary nature of Kepler-452b, to refine the size and brightness of its host star and to better pin down the size of the planet and its orbit.

The Kepler-452 system is located 1,400 light-years away in the constellation Cygnus. The research paper reporting this finding has been accepted for publication in The Astronomical Journal.

In addition to confirming Kepler-452b, the Kepler team has increased the number of new exoplanet candidates by 521 from their analysis of observations conducted from May 2009 to May 2013, raising the number of planet candidates detected by the Kepler mission to 4,696. Candidates require follow-up observations and analysis to verify they are actual planets.

Twelve of the new planet candidates have diameters between one to two times that of Earth, and orbit in their star's habitable zone. Of these, nine orbit stars that are similar to our sun in size and temperature.

"We've been able to fully automate our process of identifying planet candidates, which means we can finally assess every transit signal in the entire Kepler dataset quickly and uniformly," said Jeff Coughlin, Kepler scientist at the SETI Institute in Mountain View, California, who led the analysis of a new candidate catalog. "This gives astronomers a statistically sound population of planet candidates to accurately determine the number of small, possibly rocky planets like Earth in our Milky Way galaxy."

These findings, presented in the seventh Kepler Candidate Catalog, will be submitted for publication in The Astrophysical Journal. These findings are derived from data publicly available on the NASA Exoplanet Archive.

Scientists now are producing the last catalog based on the original Kepler mission's four-year data set. The final analysis will be conducted using sophisticated software that is increasingly sensitive to the tiny telltale signatures of Earth-size planets.

Ames manages the Kepler and K2 missions for NASA's Science Mission Directorate. NASA's Jet Propulsion Laboratory in Pasadena, California, managed Kepler mission development. Ball Aerospace & Technologies Corporation operates the flight system with support from the Laboratory for Atmospheric and Space Physics at the University of Colorado in Boulder.

For more information about the Kepler mission, visit: http://www.nasa.gov/kepler

A related feature story about other potentially habitable planets is online at: http://www.nasa.gov/jpl/finding-another -earth

www.nasa.gov/press-release/nasa-kepler-mission-discovers-bigger-older-cousin-to-earth

-end-

Felicia Chou

Washington DC 202-358-0257 felicia.chou@nasa.gov

Michele Johnson

Ames Research Center, Moffett Field, Calif. 650-604-6982 michele.johnson@nasa.gov

Links:

Briefing materials

Reporter package

Media Advisory

Last Updated: April 5, 2016

Editor: Michele Johnson

Tags: Ames Research Center, Distant Planets, Jet Propulsion Laboratory, Kepler and K2, Universe

The next day, news media giant CNN picked up the story. Chou and Johnson's metaphor of "Earth's bigger, older cousin" was so good that the network reproduced it in its headline. The CNN reporter, Michael Pearson, also reproduced the concept of a "habitable zone" of a solar system in his lead paragraph and then interviewed one of the NASA researchers who was quoted in the press release. There were inevitably other researchers who could discuss the discovery, but Jenkins was clearly prepared for reporters' questions, and so NASA effectively signaled his availability by featuring him in the press release. It's not that Pearson was lazy; there are just very few astrophysicists in a journalist's network, and Jenkins contributed to the discovery. The interview allowed Pearson to ask a few follow-up questions, but a number of quotes from the press release are interwoven into his reporting. Beyond the interview with Jenkins, Pearson departs from the press release principally at the end of his report when he offers helpful background about the Kepler mission and what lies ahead for NASA researchers.

NASA finds 'Earth's bigger, older cousin'

By Michael Pearson, CNN

Updated 9:35 AM ET, Fri July 24, 2015

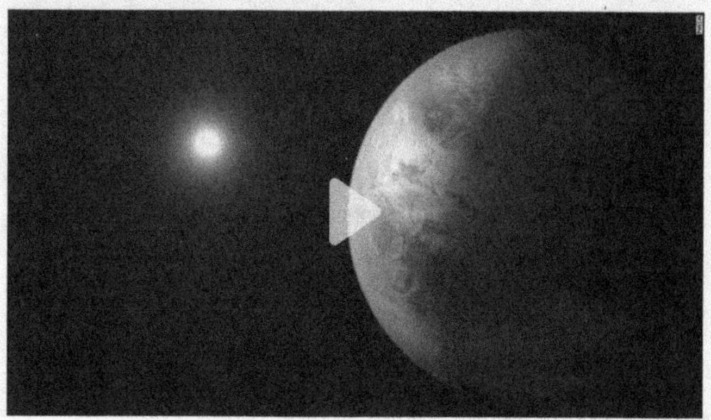

NASA Finds "Earth's Bigger, Older Cousin"
By Michael Pearson, CNN

Updated 9:35 AM ET, Fri July 24, 2015

NASA said Thursday that its Kepler spacecraft has spotted "Earth's bigger, older cousin": the first nearly Earth-size planet to be found in the habitable zone of a star similar to our own.

Though NASA can't say for sure whether the planet is rocky like ours or has water and air, it's the closest match yet found.

"Today, Earth is a little less lonely," Kepler researcher Jon Jenkins said.

The planet, Kepler-452b, is about 1,400 light-years from Earth in the constellation Cygnus. It's about 60 percent bigger than Earth, NASA says, and is located in its star's habitable zone—the region where life-sustaining liquid water is possible on the surface of a planet.

A visitor there would experience gravity about twice that of Earth's, and planetary scientists say the odds of it having a rocky surface are "better than even."

While it's a bit farther from its star than Earth is from the sun, its star is brighter, so the planet gets about the same amount of energy from its star as Earth does from the sun. And that sunlight would be very similar to Earth's, Jenkins said.

The planet "almost certainly has an atmosphere," Jenkins said, although scientists can't say what it's made of. But if the assumptions of planetary geologists are correct, he said, Kepler-452b's atmosphere would probably be thicker than Earth's, and it would have active volcanoes.

It takes 385 days for the planet to orbit its star, very similar to Earth's 365-day year, NASA said. And because it's spent so long orbiting in this zone—6 billion years—it's had plenty of time to brew life, Jenkins said.

"That's substantial opportunity for life to arise, should all the necessary ingredients and conditions for life exist on this planet," he said in a statement.

Before the discovery of this planet, one called Kepler-186f was considered the most Earthlike, according to NASA. That planet, no more than a tenth larger than Earth, is about 500 light-years away from us. But it gets only about a third of the energy from its star as Earth does from the sun, and noon there would look similar to the evening sky here, NASA says.

The $600 million Kepler mission launched in 2009 with a goal to survey a portion of the Milky Way for habitable planets.

From a vantage point 64 million miles from Earth, it scans the light from distant stars, looking for almost imperceptible drops in a star's brightness, suggesting a planet has passed in front of it.

It has discovered more than 1,000 planets. Twelve of those, including Kepler-425b, have been less than twice the size of Earth and in the habitable zones of the stars they orbit.

Missions are being readied to move scientists closer to the goal of finding yet more planets and cataloging their atmospheres and other characteristics.

In 2017, NASA plans to launch a planet-hunting satellite called TESS that will be able to provide scientists with more detail on the size, mass and atmospheres of planets circling distant stars.

The next year, the James Webb Space Telescope will go up. That platform, NASA says, will provide astonishing insights into other worlds, including their color, seasonal differences, weather and even the potential presence of vegetation.

4

THE OP-ED AND BLOG

PRINCIPLES

Reaching Constituencies

While press releases are covert in their interpretation of information, op-eds and blogs are overt. Indeed, because press releases ultimately leave journalists to publish the information they contain, they do not enable you to directly advocate, offer policy recommendations, or communicate the angle you desire. In short, your ideas can get lost in translation. Op-eds and blogs allow you to bypass a middleman and present your ideas to your target audience directly. Success relies heavily on your ability to persuade.

Today, the term "op-ed" is often used synonymously with "opinion pieces." The term, however, has a more specific meaning: it refers to the page of a newspaper that is "opposite the editorial page." Editorials are commentary articles that reflect the opinion of a newspaper's editorial board. The editorial board meets on a regular basis to discuss and debate issues of the day before publishing its recommendations and opinions. Also known as "staff editorials," these editorial board pieces do not have a byline because they reflect the consensus of the editorial board, even though they are typically written by a single editorial writer (and disagreement among these board members is frequent). Print newspapers typically only have space to print three or four op-eds a day, and one or two of these spots are often filled by regular columnists who are commissioned by (and often serve on) the editorial board. However, a newspaper's website allows it to publish many more op-ed submissions. These submissions can take on different forms, but they come from members of the general public, some highly distinguished but others with no public profile at all. Indeed, some news publications like the *Guardian* publish dozens of op-eds each day on their website, the majority of which do not actually appear in the physical newspaper.

In any such publication, the editorial board and its members carefully curate what is published—which op-eds they choose. It is this curatorial discretion by the editors—and the opinions they express in their staff editorials—that give publications their ideological reputations. It's also one reason why liberals lean toward the *New York Times* and conservatives gravitate to the *Wall Street Journal* or *New York Post*. This background about how each news publication works is important to bear in mind because it will inform where you may send your own op-eds. With what target audience will your message strike a chord?

The near-costless access to extra web space has also produced the evolution of weblogs (known as "blogs"), where individuals may self-publish their ideas and opinions without the filter imposed by editors. Naturally, there is a trade-off. A blog you self-publish will not benefit from two of a newspaper's greatest assets: the expertise of its editors who provide feedback and the consumption of an already established readership. In recent years, some blogs have grown far beyond the content provided by their original bloggers into destinations where many external commentators post articles. While some of these blogs are relatively open to new submissions, others impose filters much like newspapers. And much like newspapers, these websites feature their own unique readerships, the attributes of which may be related to a shared ideology, subject matter, or region of interest.

Despite all this diversity in the world of publishing commentary, nearly all publications share a common set of expectations for op-ed or blog contributions. These articles are expected to be tightly written—typically ranging from 600 to 1,200 words—arguments about a specific subject matter. In short, they should be punchy, coherent contributions to a single debate that you are qualified to enter. This may entail taking a new angle on what everyone is talking about or raising to prominence an issue that no one is talking about. It will almost certainly entail addressing a subject matter of which you have extensive knowledge or a practical acquaintance.

Structure

Op-eds and press releases share a number of fundamentals. Like press releases, op-eds and blogs begin with a clear "lead," generally follow inverted pyramid structure, and can be enhanced by hyperlinked materials. However, while press releases rely on journalists to translate their information into publishable articles, op-eds are expected to be polished pieces when submitted. Accordingly, they do not have the luxury of unrestricted word counts and the certainty of self-publication. Rather, authors must adhere to external editorial preferences, compete for publication, and grasp a reader's attention. This influences the character of the text you produce in several ways.

A LEAD THAT POPS

For every op-ed a newspaper publishes in print, hundreds are turned away. (While blog editors have far more space at their disposal, they have limited time and are concerned with engaging their readerships.) This means that your contribution not only needs to be something that will attract readers who are distracted by myriad other things in their lives but also needs to attract editors who have limited time and an abundance of other options. Your lead sentence or paragraph needs to "pop," and it needs to do so quickly. The crux of your argument needs to go at the very top. And if it does not, there must be a compelling introduction or headline that sustains your readers' attention. One way to tell whether your lead is interesting is by asking the following questions:

- Will many people disagree with me?
- Has this contention never or rarely been made before?
- Is this an argument people would want to share with others?
- Will this change the way people think or violate their intuition?

The more times you can say "yes," the more your lead (and your article) will pop.

EVERY PARAGRAPH MATTERS

You must assume that your reader is exceptionally busy with countless demands on her attention. Imagine that when she stumbles upon your op-ed or blog, she is in a busy coffee shop, music is playing, she is people watching, exchanging emails with her boss, trading texts with her child's caregiver, bombarded by internet advertising, all while waiting for the barista to yell that her iced oat milk latté is ready for pickup. As soon as your article gets boring, she will move to the next article or shift her gaze to see if the barista is working on her order. You do not have the luxury of a long windup. Remind yourself that your opinion is more important than where it comes from (your thought process is typically not worth rehashing). Get to the point. And tell your busy, attention-deficient reader why she should care about this issue that you have spent so much time studying or promoting. What are the stakes? How does it affect her life? What are the consequences of ignorance or mindless latté-sipping?

Consider two pieces of advice directly from William Strunk, Jr., and E. B. White's *The Elements of Style*[1]:

> First, use definite, specific, concrete language. Prefer the specific to the general, the definite to the vague, the concrete to the abstract. Instead of "A period of unfavorable weather set in," write "It rained every day for a week." Instead of "He showed his satisfaction as he took possession of his well-earned reward," write "He grinned as he pocketed the coin." The greatest writers—Homer, Dante, Shakespeare—are effective largely because they deal in particulars and report the details that matter. Their words call up pictures.
>
> Second, omit needless words. Vigorous writing is concise. A sentence should contain no unnecessary words, a paragraph no unnecessary sentences, for the same reason that a drawing should have no unnecessary lines and a machine no

1. Strunk, W., & White, E. B. (2000). *The elements of style* (fourth edition). New York, NY: Pearson Longman, 21–23.

> unnecessary part. This requires not that the writer make all sentences short, avoid all detail and treat subjects only in outline, but that every word tell.

USE A NEWS PEG

Good op-eds are rarely non sequiturs. They are relevant to the intended reader. In print, newspapers seek out op-eds that directly engage what their news pages are covering. It promotes greater coherency in their publication and offers alternative angles on the day's events. And while blogs are not constrained by news pages, they too want contributions that tap into debates that they are hosting and conversations trending elsewhere. As a result, successful op-eds and blogs usually have a news peg—a reference to a current event, phenomenon, or debate—placed in the first paragraph or two. And these pegs are usually subjects that the publication has already been discussing. (This is also a way to select a particular publication. If your subject matter is in their news or opinion pages, it is more likely that they will take an interest in further content on the topic.)

CRAFT A STORY

As I emphasize in the previous chapter, stories are often more effective than logical deduction. Drawing on the evolution of the brain and the last half-century of US elections, in *The Political Brain: The Role of Emotion in Deciding the Fate of the Nation*, Drew Westen[2] shows that people vote based on their emotions, not on a dispassionate, rational assessment of

2. Westen, D. (2007). *The political brain: The role of emotion in deciding the fate of the nation*. New York, NY: Public Affairs.

policy issues. "In politics," he writes, "when reason and emotion collide, emotion invariably wins." Naturally, I am not suggesting that you force stories when they do not exist or do not lend themselves to the argument you are developing. And do not allow injections of emotion to distract from the ostensible reason of your claims, either. However, strive to craft narratives that help readers understand the news from your perspective and remember your main contention.

EMPHASIZE WHAT IS SUBSTANTIVELY NEW

News and commentary publications grant special leniency to distinguished contributors. While luminaries want the prestige and reach associated with certain publications, those same publications desire the status and readership that an op-ed from a luminary will generate. Accordingly, editors will tolerate more mundane and rhetorical commentaries from a Member of Congress or Parliament than they otherwise would from a young writer without a public profile. In a 2017 column, "Tips for Aspiring Op-Ed Writers," *New York Times* columnist Bret Stephens writes that editors will also demand more novelty from the unknown author: "Young writers with no particular expertise or name recognition are likelier to get published by following an 80–20 rule: 80 percent new information; 20 percent opinion."[3]

REFERENCES

For a very long time, newspapers made it challenging to cite sources of information. In the interest of clarity and style, newspapers simply do not use in-text citations, nor do they

3. Stephens, B. (2017). Tips for aspiring op-ed writers. *New York Times*, August 25.

permit footnotes. So writers were forced to awkwardly note sources and thicken their prose with references like "according to a report released by the Center for Responsive Politics today." The inconvenience of such citations occasionally justified their omission from commentary articles and news articles alike. This is no longer the case. The digital publication of news and commentary permits easily citing others' work or ideas by hyperlinking your passing in-text references to external analysis, tweets, reporting, profile, or video. Blogs are now multicolored with the sheer quantity of hyperlinks embedded in their text. And publications look with favor upon contributions that link to their earlier work. Just make sure you do not overdo it. Ultimately, your article is about your contribution and argument, not the state of the supporting literature.

While ensuring the execution of these fundamentals, a special kind of clarity is essential. If you are writing an op-ed or blog, you are likely soliciting the interest and support of a relatively general readership—one without expertise in (or possibly an acquaintance with) your subject matter. Accordingly, it is imperative that you use language any reader of your targeted publication can understand. Avoid acronyms, abbreviations, and jargon. Embrace simple, accessible language that, rather than demonstrating how much more you know, makes your reader feel a command over the topic matter sufficient to join the discussion you're initiating. Clarity is enhanced by succinct, basic sentence structure and by the incorporation of examples that illustrate your ideas with known concepts or convenient references. In the interest of clarity, sometimes you may feel like you must orient the reader before she or he can truly appreciate your argument, particularly when it pertains to complicated subject matters. Resist this feeling. The challenge of drafting a strong lead and opening is to deliver your argument in a digestible manner, even if this means without the full context. Place this context later in the article as a springboard to your more nuanced ideas and examples. Otherwise, you risk losing your reader's attention before you've even presented your point.

Outreach

No matter how well written and interesting your op-ed or blog is, it will not be externally published without the approval of an editor. This is why, more than any other media form, op-eds require attention to the idiosyncrasies of the media organizations with which you wish to work. They also require careful outreach to the editors of the publication. Nearly all welcome unsolicited op-eds and blogs via web forms or emails. These messages are as integral to being published as the actual text of your work, so they merit special focus here.

Before we discuss the substance of your outreach, it is worth conducting a little armchair psychology about news publication editors. Editors are typically former reporters and commentary writers themselves, who are keen but nonexpert observers of current affairs. This means that they are finicky about clear writing and confident that if they can't understand or appreciate your subject matter, no one else will. Beyond this professional self-assurance, there are occupational hazards. Editors are typically overworked and pressurized by tight deadlines. One editor, and possibly one other subeditor, is tasked with sifting through the aforementioned hundreds of submissions received each day. The daunting challenge of identifying, editing, and publishing the juiciest contributions before their shelf lives expire in the news cycle makes these editors rushed and brutally selective. In short, they are pressed and stressed and don't want to be messed around.

As a result, your outreach to editors should

- be extremely brief and clear (There is no need for pleasantries; just get to the point.);
- adhere to any requirements expressed in the online submission instructions;
- keep the pitch to one sentence—typically your lead sentence;
- unless otherwise specified, include a polite greeting, pitch summary, brief biography, the full text of your submission (without attachments), and nothing else.

This makes it easy for the editor to skim and identify the pitch and suggests to the editor that you can follow instructions and will be a cooperative contributor. Editors do not like attachments because they take time to open and run the risk of downloading viruses. This chapter's Paragon will offer an example of outreach to an op-ed editor.

Because editors typically want a clear news peg, timing and speed are essential. When events happen, many other people will submit op-eds that are hastily written to apply their ideas to the subject matter. If you can anticipate such events, it may be advisable to draft an "evergreen" op-ed—one that you may send out when its moment in the spotlight arises. Alternatively, you may write the bulk of your argument and adapt the hook to breaking news when the time comes, with minimal work. The quicker turnaround will allow you to submit before anyone else.

If you are fortunate enough to be selected, be a model contributor. First, editors are professionals. They have read and edited countless articles and are as interested as you are in publishing top work. So when they provide feedback, accept it. Unless there is a misunderstanding or their suggested changes lead to inaccuracies or substantive differences, their suggestions are likely to strengthen the delivery of your ideas. Second, editors have long memories, and they remember contributors who are slow to reply, resistant to feedback, or just plain divas. So if there is even a remote chance that you may one day wish to publish an op-ed or blog again anywhere (editors occasionally change publications), it's best to secure a good rapport with your editor. The rewards can be great. When editors consider so many hundreds of contributions, it is an enormous advantage to be able to directly contact an editor with whom you have a strong relationship and make a more personal pitch outside of the automated system.

On occasions when you are rejected—and you will be rejected—don't be dismayed. Most op-eds are turned away, often without the dignity of a formal rejection message. Continue submitting to other publications, and continue to refine the clarity, argumentation, and appeal of your ideas. On occasions when an op-ed is not placed—and there will be many fruitless efforts—don't be hard on yourself. There will be other opportunities with new events in world affairs. You might also aim for lower-tier publications, where there is less competition and, if selected, the editors may be willing to advise on how to improve your work. These interactions are priceless. Keep writing, and maintain your confidence.

PRACTITIONER

Peter Canellos *is the editor-at-large for POLITICO, where he previously served as Executive Editor. Previously, he spent five years as the editor of the editorial page for* The Boston Globe, *for which he wrote for 26 years, including a period as the Washington, DC bureau chief. I asked him to share his advice about preparing blogs and op-eds. Here are his thoughts.*

> The most important thing to remember when writing an op-ed is that it's a work of journalism, not public relations. Everyone with a cause yearns to give voice to it in a newspaper or online opinion site, but editors will quickly suss out which ones are fresh and interesting and which are self-serving promotions, however worthy the cause.
>
> Let's just stipulate that an organization dedicated to promoting research into curing a deadly disease is eager for money and has a lot of sad stories to tell. But simply explaining that the Q virus is deadly and shatters families and that it's, therefore, important to support research efforts doesn't make for a satisfactory op-ed. In most cases, it isn't revealing anything that readers don't already know, making a clever argument, or providing information on which people can act. It's more like a public appeal, an advertisement, and all but the most copy-hungry news organizations will reject it.
>
> Now let's suppose that an obscure provision of Obamacare is giving insurers reasons to stop funding a crucial vaccine that protects against the Q virus. That could be the germ of a real op-ed—a weighing of policy priorities that engages readers and addresses an important question facing the government. It's a

surprising tale, even if the underlying opinion—that an organization dedicated to curing a disease wants to get more funding to prevent it—isn't all that different than in the first example.

Keep in mind that editors will judge op-ed submissions in light of their journalistic mission—essentially, to provide the most interesting pieces for their readers. The op-ed page isn't a public bulletin board: it's a part of the news organization's effort to enlighten and engage its audience. The pieces that are best written, most surprising to readers, and most powerful in their argument are the ones that will be chosen.

A few dos and don'ts:

1. It usually doesn't matter if the writer is the head of the organization that's submitting it, so writing a piece and then putting it under the boss's name isn't an advantage unless the boss is a major public figure. The best pieces are the ones with real spontaneity and originality; something that's written to satisfy a boss's request will almost certainly have neither one. If the boss wants to write an op-ed, he or she should do it themselves, and it should reflect their own unique perspective, even if an aide helps with the editing. Better still, if there's someone in the organization with a real passion or spark, let them write the op-ed and put it under their own byline.

2. Dual bylines are a red flag for some editors. Really, how many great pieces of writing have been produced by two authors? Submitting a piece by two authors—usually the heads of two organizations, seeking to combine their clout—all but advertises the fact that the piece is self-serving and has probably been hashed over by underlings.

3. Don't gratuitously reference colleagues whose names mean nothing to readers. Many academics either feel obliged to credit ideas to others in an excess of generosity or, perhaps, because they think it will give greater weight to the piece. It won't. It will likely just slow it down and confuse readers who think they're supposed to be familiar with these outside sources. (On the other hand, if citing information from a statistical study, it's important to cite the source so readers can discern if there's a bias.)

4. If editors express interest in a piece but ask for changes, try hard to accommodate them. Their interest and that of the writer are actually aligned—getting the most eyeballs for the piece. Too often, though, writers for advocacy organizations—think of that group promoting research into the Q virus—are so wrapped up in the rightness of their cause that they refuse to make changes to the piece, even to sharpen its argument or remove unnecessary background.

Remember that a powerful op-ed changes the world. The greatest manifestos—think of Martin Luther King, Jr., and the "Letter from Birmingham Jail"—are essentially op-eds. So don't hold back, and don't forget that you're addressing yourself to the public and appealing to the public interest. Be lively. Be colorful. Show your passion with vivid images and powerful turns of phrase. Like Dr. King, go to that mountaintop, and the readers will follow.

PARAGON

Jordan Ellenberg is a professor of mathematics at the University of Wisconsin-Madison. His biography lists a number of research interests in arithmetic algebraic geometry that most of us have never encountered—nonabelian Iwasawa theory, pro-p group theory, automorphic forms, to name but a few. While a very distinguished mathematician, he does not have a widely known public profile. However, he is able to convert his most sophisticated ideas into plain English that can reach people who last sat through a math class in high school. He is the author of a book, How Not to Be Wrong: The Power of Mathematical Thinking, *but also an exceptionally clear and approachable op-ed in* The New York Times. *At its core, this article is about highly sophisticated mathematical algorithms, but he uses simple, succinct language and an excellent metaphor about the Volkswagen emissions scandal to describe the way that Wisconsin Republicans used mathematics to turn a split partisan state into a Republican stronghold. In doing so, he connects his advanced and esoteric expertise to a subject matter at the center of public and political attention.*

Preceding the text of Ellenberg's op-ed is a template for an outreach email. As a convenient example, I drafted this in the fabricated voice of Jordan Ellenberg to The New York Times. *Note that it is always an advantage to build a relationship with editors, such that you may send your pitch to the editor himself or herself, rather than to an impersonal, general mailbox. However, I have drafted this template as if Mr. Ellenberg did not have a preexisting relationship with the editor or publication. The text reflects the published edition of Ellenberg's article. However, it is likely that the newspaper's capable editorial staff substantially edited it.*

SUBJECT: OP-ED: How Computers Turned Gerrymandering Into a Science

> Dear Editor,
>
> Below, please find my proposed commentary about the mathematics behind the Supreme Court case on gerrymandering in Wisconsin. (962 words)
>
> Thank you for your consideration.
>
> My warmest regards,
>
> Jordan Ellenberg
>
> mobile: 608.555.1212
>
> SUMMARY:
>
> Gerrymandering used to be an art, but advanced computation has made it a science. Wisconsin's Republican legislators, after their victory in the census year of 2010, tried out map after map, tweak after tweak. They ran each potential map through computer algorithms that tested its performance in a wide range of political climates. The map they adopted is

precisely engineered to assure Republican control in all but the most extreme circumstances. The map is an "outlier"—so far outside the ordinary run of things that it can't be mistaken for a map without partisan purpose.

BIO:

Jordan Ellenberg is a professor of mathematics at the University of Wisconsin and the author of *How Not to Be Wrong: The Power of Mathematical Thinking.*

The New York Times

Opinion

GRAY MATTER

How Computers Turned Gerrymandering Into a Science

By Jordan Ellenberg

By JORDAN ELLENBERG OCT. 6, 2017

MADISON, Wis.—About as many Democrats live in Wisconsin as Republicans do. But you wouldn't know it from the Wisconsin State Assembly, where Republicans hold 65 percent of the seats, a bigger majority than Republican legislators enjoy in conservative states like Texas and Kentucky.

The United States Supreme Court is trying to understand how that happened. On Tuesday, the justices heard oral arguments in Gill v. Whitford, reviewing a three-judge panel's determination that Wisconsin's Republican-drawn district map is so flagrantly gerrymandered that it denies Wisconsinites their full right to vote. A long list of elected officials, representing both parties, have filed briefs asking the justices to uphold the panel's ruling.

Other people don't see a problem. Politics, they say, is a game where whoever's ahead gets to change the rules on the fly. It's about winning, not being fair.

But this isn't just a politics story; it's also a technology story. Gerrymandering used to be an art, but advanced computation has made it a science. Wisconsin's Republican legislators, after their victory in the census year of 2010, tried out map after map, tweak after tweak. They ran each potential map through computer algorithms that tested its performance in a wide range of political climates. The map they adopted is precisely engineered to assure Republican control in all but the most extreme circumstances.

In a gerrymandered map, you concentrate opposing voters in a few districts where you lose big, and win the rest by modest margins. But it's risky to count on a lot of close wins, which can easily flip to close losses. Justice Sandra Day O'Connor thought this risk meant the Supreme Court didn't need to step in. In a 1986 case, she wrote that "there is good reason to think political gerrymandering is a self-limiting enterprise" since "an overambitious gerrymander can lead to disaster for the legislative majority."

Back then, she may have been right. But today's computing power has blown away the self-limiting nature of the enterprise, as it has with so many other limits. A new paper by a team of scientists at Duke paints a startling picture of the way the Wisconsin district map protects Republicans from risk. Remember the Volkswagen scandal? Volkswagen installed software in its diesel cars to fool regulators into thinking the engines were meeting emissions standards. The software detected when it was being tested, and only then did it turn on the antipollution system. The Wisconsin district map is a similarly audacious piece of engineering.

When the overall Republican vote share in the state is 50 percent or more, the authors of the paper show, the map behaves much like an unbiased one. But when the map is tested by an electorate that leans Democratic, its special features kick in, maintaining a healthy Republican majority against the popular headwind. To gain control of the State Assembly, the authors estimate, Wisconsin Democrats would have to beat Republicans by eight to ten points, a margin rarely achieved in statewide elections by either party in this evenly split state. As a mathematician, I'm impressed. As a Wisconsin voter, I feel a little ill.

Republican legislators argue that any Wisconsin map will look biased, because Democratic voters tend to congregate in big cities like Milwaukee and Madison. That packs the Democratic half of the state into a small cluster of districts. "Why are you gerrymandering yourselves?" they ask.

They're partly right. The clustering of Democrats in cities does indeed give the Republicans an edge. But it's a much smaller advantage than the turbo-boost the current map provides, as the Duke paper demonstrates. The main tool in the Duke paper is a method called the "Markov chain Monte Carlo" algorithm. Starting from the current Wisconsin district map, it makes a sequence of random changes, swapping wards from one district to an adjacent one, carrying out a "random walk" through the set of all possible maps. Completely unconstrained changes would create crazy-looking districts, so it weights its changes in favor of traditional districting criteria.

Few if any of these maps provide the Republicans the firewall against a Democratic electorate that the Wisconsin district map does. In other words, the map is an "outlier"—so far outside the ordinary run of things that it can't be mistaken for a map without partisan purpose. It's an outlier in another way, too: Research by the political scientist Jowei Chen suggests that the Wisconsin district map does much worse on traditional districting criteria than neutral maps do, despite the Wisconsin Constitution's requirement that districts be "in as compact form as practicable."

Outlier detection is a critical part of data analysis, and mathematicians have gotten really good at it by now. That's the good news about advanced computation: You can use it to make electoral mischief, but you can also use it to detect and measure that mischief. It's not math versus democracy; it's math versus math, with democracy at stake.

If the Supreme Court sides with the three-judge panel that blocked the Wisconsin map, some liberals foresee an end to gerrymandering, while some conservatives imagine a districting process that is the purview of legislatures being completely usurped by the courts. Both sides of Gill v. Whitford agree: This is a momentous case with major implications for American democracy.

But what if it's not? The panel's standards for determining impermissible gerrymandering are hard to meet except in the most egregious cases. Judges empowered by an anti-gerrymandering precedent from the Supreme Court will blunt the worst cases, but won't end gerrymandering. There will be many cases, maybe most of them, where it's impossible, no matter how much math you do, to tell the difference between innocuous decision making and a scheme—like Wisconsin's—designed to protect one party from voters who might prefer the other.

THE BRIEFING

PRINCIPLES

Reaching Stakeholders

With briefings, your writing becomes animated by image and sound. The live presentation naturally compels attention in ways that simple text never will. During a "performance," there is a sense of tension between the presenter and the audience—a sense of obligation to follow the speaker, an urgency to listen lest you miss fleeting details, the pressure to connect and captivate the audience, the added stimulation of audio and visual elements.

But with greater resources come greater expectations and greater risks. Indeed, from live speakers, we expect style to accompany substance in a way we cannot from an op-ed or executive summary. And that style—delivered live and thus without the opportunity to revise—is just as capable of distracting our listeners as it is of committing their attention. In this light, there is a performative aspect to oral presentation. It may come as no surprise, then, that the best advice I have ever received about delivering briefings came from someone who specialized in voice training for actors—Elise Morrison.

Much of this chapter is derived from the guidance she offered during my time as a Harvard University lecturer about tone and body language. The focus then was on lecturing, but many of the underlying principles apply equally to delivering briefings.

Actors and entertainers understand that people's attention can be erratic, quite generally. This is particularly true of those listening to a briefing. Boardrooms typically seat a number of interested stakeholders for a focused meeting. Because many board meetings are invitation-only, these are exclusive venues to influence people with direct power or a direct line to those who possess it. Sometimes, the briefing is for the executive her- or himself. Such individuals typically have little time, which is why you may not otherwise be invited to circulate a full memo or report. Rather, you are being invited to present a coherent narrative of your ideas, address questions about them, and defend them against criticism from people who want to advance their own agendas and priorities.

While some of these meetings are purely for the purpose of information sharing, others come with an action-oriented agenda. Do we fund this new program? What recommendation do we make to the secretary? How shall we vote tomorrow? The briefing is an efficient way to deliver evidence and conclusions in a very short period of time. It requires attendees to prepare very little and allows them to follow up with questions for the purpose of clarification, evaluation, or interpretation.

Because briefings are performed live and in person, they are subject to the three principal registers of interpersonal communication: content (the substance of your message), tone (your vocal communication), and body language (your nonverbal communication). I will address each of these sequentially. However, it is first worth acknowledging that your choices—across each of these registers—should always be with the audience in mind. The strongest presenters understand that audiences cannot be modified, but your message and delivery can. Accordingly, strong presenters are versatile; they are able to communicate diverse messages to diverse audiences, all while maintaining authenticity. This takes time and practice to hone, but you can start by beginning your preparation for any briefing by inquiring about the nature of your audience:

- Who is my audience? And accordingly, what will they seek to derive from my presentation and remarks? What will stimulate them?
- What is my audience likely to know about my subject? And accordingly, at what level can I speak without losing members of the audience to confusion or boredom? What details may I omit under the assumption that they are known?
- What biases do members of my audience likely hold? Do they have a preexisting perspective on the topic? And accordingly, where can we find common ground that facilitates persuasion?
- What are my audience's expectations of me? And accordingly, to the extent that these expectations are helpful, how can I fulfill them? To the extent that these are unhelpful, how can I swiftly challenge them to earn their open consideration?
- What is the learning and discursive style of my audience? Are they likely to frequently interrupt with

> questions and disputes? Are they listeners who will wait for me to conclude my remarks before engaging?

This point was reinforced in my exchanges with Mike Morell, the former acting director and deputy director of the US Central Intelligence Agency (CIA). Over a 33-year career in national intelligence, Morell briefed four sitting US presidents hundreds of times—including daily intelligence briefings to President George W. Bush and regular National Security Council briefings to President Barack Obama. "You have to know your audience," he told me. "With President Obama, I knew he was not going to interrupt and ask questions until the end. He's sitting there and taking it all in. [George W.] Bush was more likely to spar with me—always constructively, but he interrupted with questions."

Morell adapted his presentation style and content to accommodate the chief executive. "When I was preparing to go to the WH and I had a presentation, the junior analysts would write talking points for me," he said. "About 95 percent of the time, the talking points were worthless. I would read them and set them aside and never look at them again. I would then prepare for the briefing by asking the questions that the talking points brought to mind, which I knew the executive would want to be answered. . . . The most frequent thing I said in my office when preparing for a meeting downtown was: 'That's not addressing the question I asked. Don't answer that. Here's what the president will want to know.' There is a tendency to go somewhere you're comfortable, rather than put yourself in the audience's shoes."

To make sure you do the same, Morell insisted that his analysts write out their presentations before preparing slides or making remarks. "Briefings are extraordinarily dangerous," he said, "because it's very difficult for the listener to *hear* logic flaws. When you're reading, it's much easier to *see* them. At CIA, we don't give a briefing without first writing down what you want to say. When you write, you're forced to get the logic right and you are able to let other people review it." On the one hand, writing the presentation in advance reveals the importance of text even with oral communications media. On the other hand, Morell acknowledges that advance writing must be prepared with oral delivery in mind. First, we do not write in the same manner we speak; the best presenters speak to audiences conversationally to develop a credible human connection. So your prepared materials should be adapted to what will sound the most natural. And second, presenters should never feel obligated to adhere to the text. Otherwise, the presentation will feel scripted and unnatural, and you will be more concerned with following your prepared remarks and less concerned with communicating clearly. "For every briefing I gave President Obama, I practiced two or three times," Morell said. "I didn't want to take any paper with me, but memorizing is the worst thing you can do."

Content

With content, clarity is paramount, but obstacles abound. Briefings—any oral forms of communication really—provide strong temptations to digress. This can be due to distractions created by unsolicited questions or by your reactions to the audible and visible responses you receive from your audience in real time (skepticism, laughter, yawning, etc.). Because written media are not consumed while they are produced, there is ample time for self-editing. This tool is unavailable to oral presenters unless you are being recorded and subject to postproduction techniques. Rather, oral presenters must think on the fly, which is why question-and-answer periods are equally important as—and often more revealing than—carefully scripted presentations.

As you prepare your presentation and anticipate lines of questioning, you must balance your own goals with those of your listeners. This is what it means to be an audience-focused presenter. The natural first question you must ask yourself—as you would before communicating in any media—is what precisely you want your audience to remember from your presentation. Therefore, be very clear about your goal, and communicate its message up front. In doing so, consider the well-researched effects of "framing," which affects decisions between choices that are effectively identical. A number of experiments have shown that focusing people's attention on desirable prospects generates a higher likelihood of selection than focusing on risks with the same prospects, like 90 percent employment versus 10 percent unemployment or 95 percent survival versus 5 percent mortality.[1]

A further consideration is terminology. In *The Political Mind*, George Lakoff fosters an awareness of the associations that certain words create:

> *If health care is framed as "health insurance," then it will be seen through an insurance frame, and the policy will fit that frame: it*

1. McNeil, B. J., Pauker, S. G., Sox, H. C., & Tversky, A. (1982). On the elicitation of preferences for alternative therapies. *New England Journal of Medicine, 306*, 1259–1262; Quattrone, G., & Tversky, A. (1988). Contrasting rational and psychological analyses of political choice, *American Political Science Review, 82*(3), 719–736, doi:10.2307/1962487; Kahneman, D., & Anderson, Norman B. (2003). A perspective on judgment and choice. *American Psychologist, 58*(9), 697–720.

> *will be a business, with profits, administrative costs, premiums, actuaries, outsourcing, care criteria, denial of care to maximize profits, and many people not buying insurance even if it is required by law. Whereas if healthcare is seen as protection—on a par with police and fire protection, food safety, and so on—then it becomes part of the moral mission of government, where the role of government is protection and empowerment, which in turn is based on a morality of empathy and responsibility. In this case, policy proposals will look more like Medicare for all.*[2]

Accordingly, consider the words you wish to use for critical statements and repeated references in advance of your briefing. Practice using those words and phrases so that their incorporation into your everyday speech ensures their use in your interactions with people thereafter.

Remember that most listeners will approach your briefings by asking, "What do I have to gain from this?" and "Why should I listen to you?" You want to address such questions directly and as practically as possible at the very start. Explain to your audience what they will gain from giving you their attention. Offer an overview of your remarks. And explain how you know what you know. Assert your credibility. Your opening slides or remarks should always cover the following (in flexible order):

- an overview of your presentation, to orient your audience
- the impetus for your presentation, to align your goals with those of your audience

2. Lakoff, George (2008). *The political mind: Why you can't understand 21st-century politics with an 18th-century brain.* New York, NY: Penguin, 67.

- a description of what is at stake, to show why your audience should listen
- a depiction of your background or methods (if it is not clear), to establish credibility
- a succinct outline of your argument, to clarify your principal message to all

After you've presented the bottom line, you may choose to modify your delivery according to subsequent questions that reflect the audience's outlook.

There are alternative approaches as well. Mike Morell, the former acting director of the CIA, advocates for storytelling. "I have received more briefings than I've ever given," he said. "Four or five a day, and the vast majority of people lost me. They go through their main points: boom, boom, boom. I got lost or they digressed. The extent that you can turn your presentation into a story is very powerful; it's what Hollywood does with historical fiction: Here's the question or problem, here's how we tried to figure out the answer, here's the answer and what it means for you." Morell advocates accompanying every point of argument with a "factual nugget" of data or evidence. His former boss, General Michael Hayden, was known for making use of sports metaphors to convey his perspectives to President George W. Bush—a baseball and football enthusiast.

More stylistically, clarity in content also extends to the presentation materials you use. These must be designed and selected strategically. While new software offers ever more vivid ways to display your ideas, slide presentations also risk distraction and confusion. To maximize the impact of each slide, minimize their content. As with writing on whiteboards or chalkboards, when the presenter makes the choice to document material in writing, it suggests that such material is worth reading, remembering, and emphasizing. The greater the amount of text, the less your audience will focus on your words and the more effort they will exert to distinguish what they should take away. So make it easy. Limit the words on slides to a few (two, three, or four) short bullet points that may be read swiftly so that their elaboration comes from you. This way, the slides are the guide, not the show.

The choice about whether or not to use a slide presentation may be constrained by the venue of your briefing and the resources available. But beyond these constraints, it is principally a question of what you want your audience to take away. At their most helpful, slides do what presenters cannot otherwise do with the spoken word. First, they can deliver visualizations—in the form of graphs, figures, photographs, and/or maps—that words alone cannot. You might also show a video or play audio to the extent that doing so enhances your message. These are the truest multimedia presentations. And when used appropriately, these are welcome in almost any environment. Second, slides crystallize the principal message from each segment of your presentation and can help viewers visualize the structure of your ideas. These are most appropriate in circumstances where you are instructing, educating, and communicating information. (Doing so can also provide you, the presenter, with visual cues to relieve the need for notes.) When persuading, unless you must cite data or offer the visualizations I previously mentioned, direct interpersonal communication is often most effective. This is why politicians prefer personality and professors prefer PowerPoint.

Tone

With tone, this is a matter of how you communicate, rather than what you communicate. Each of us has personal, everyday tones that we employ in conversations, formal and informal. This everyday tone is a product of habits—some of which are conducive to public speaking, others of which are not. A helpful first step is to audit these habits so that you can improve them in the future and learn how to adapt to different speaking environments. A helpful step is to video record yourself speaking and note your tendencies. (This can be painful to watch but extraordinarily helpful.) In particular, there are five primary components of tone to consider:

1) *Volume*: Volume is a matter of how loudly you speak in relation to the size of your audience and the size of the space in which you speak. Always ensure that you are heard by all by projecting your voice. However, if you feel like you may need to shout to reach your audience, request a microphone in advance (or a smaller room). At the other extreme, measure your volume such that your volume is not so high that it drowns out all other thought.
2) *Pitch*: Pitch is a matter of where in your vocal range you choose to speak. Test out your full range. If you feel like you must strain to go higher or lower, you are out of your range. Speaking with a high pitch can sound shrill, desperate, or pleading. A recent study found that people associated lower-pitched voices with favorable personality traits more often and that voters preferred politicians with lower-pitched rather

than higher-pitched voices.[3] High pitch can also be a diagnostic of what is often called "upspeak"—the tendency to raise your pitch inflection at the end of a statement. This tends to make assertions sound like questions. (One way to ensure that you assert is to silently imagine the word "dammit" following a declarative statement.) Alternatively, speaking with low pitch can sound like you are trying too hard to be authoritative. So identify a comfortable pitch range, and be yourself. By doing so, you will also find that you better enunciate words—a critical characteristic of clarity.

3) *Rate*: Rate is a matter of how quickly or slowly you speak. Different languages and cultures have different tendencies and preferences with regard to rate. A convenient example comes from the remarkable distinction between Spanish and English. In Spanish, authority is derived from a combination of speed and impeccable enunciation. Speaking slowly risks seeming feckless and lame. However, in English, speed can suggest frantic desperation, which undermines credibility. Rather, a slower rate in English often communicates command and confidence. Your choice of rate is a balance between the authority you want to convey and the amount of material you want to cover. Just remind yourself that less is usually more.

3. Tigue, C. C., Borak, D. J., O'Connor, J. J., Schandl, C., & Feinberg, D. R. (2012). Voice pitch influences voting behavior. *Evolution and Human Behavior*, *33*(3), 210–216.

4) *Pauses*: Pauses in speech are multifunctional. Per the discussion about rate, strategic pauses can demonstrate complete control of the space you are in. To pause for a beat is the luxury of a deliberate speaker who commands the floor. And the best time to employ this luxury is when you are making or have just made a particularly important point. This is because a well-timed pause allows you to "land" your message by giving your audience time to absorb and reflect on your point. It can also jolt your audience to attention far more than a sharp rise in pitch or volume. (Have you ever fallen asleep while watching television, only to wake up when it is turned off?) Pauses are also a useful way to avoid so-called filler words—the "um," "uh," "like," "sort of," and "you know"—that emerge in moments of slight disorientation. Replace such habitual fillers with a pause, and turn your sense of internal disorder into an appearance of confidence.
5) *Vocal Variety*: Vocal variety is a matter of how often you change your pitch, rate, and volume and how often you employ a well-timed pause. Variation communicates the emotion, confidence, and enthusiasm with which you speak. Varying too often will sound erratic. A lack of variation—monotony—is sure to put your audience to sleep. Accordingly, the strategic choices you make about when and how you vary your tone constitute the nature of your performance; and as with the vocalization of a screenplay, this performance should correspond to the message you want to convey in each moment.

Body Language

Body language communicates without the use of words, slides, and tone. And as with tone, we are all subject to good and bad habits, which should also be considered in your video audit. In particular, there are five primary components of nonverbal communication to consider:

1) *Eyes*: Eye contact is an essential part of public (and private) speaking because it communicates direct engagement with your audience. In larger rooms with more people, any individual audience member will forgive you for not looking specifically at him or her. However, you will not be forgiven for only addressing one side of the room, the front row, or the notes in front of you. Shift your gaze from sentence to sentence or in moments when a statement makes a pivot in content or tone. Try to spend a few seconds with each member of the audience to whom you look; shifting too frequently can appear frenetic. If it is easier to commit to habit, you can also spread your eye contact in the shape of an M or W to cover sufficient ground.
2) *Posture*: Posture tells the audience whether you are open and confident or defensive and insecure. To maximize openness and confidence, stand upright with your shoulders back and your chin extended from your neck. Expose the full front of your body to your audience, squaring your shoulders with those whom you face. Allow your arms and hands to relax and drop loosely at your sides when you are not using your hands to gesture. To minimize defensiveness and insecurity, avoid crossing your arms, putting

your hands in your pockets, or shielding your body in any way. While it can be empowering to speak at a podium or lectern, furniture separates you from your audience. Act to remove such barriers, whether it is an empty chair or your own clasped hands.

3) *Hands*: Hands are a force of good and evil in public speaking. Top speakers use their hands to gesticulate, specify, and elaborate the content of their presentations. This is yet another reason why it is important to keep your arms uncrossed and your hands unclasped and out of your pockets. They render your presence a third dimension. However, for many people, fiddling hands are also the first manifestation of nerves. So if you know that you are prone to fiddling, minimize opportunities. Empty your pockets of change and keys that you may otherwise jingle. Don't wear loose bracelets or necklaces that you may otherwise adjust. Pull back hair that you may otherwise twist and twirl. Put down the slide remote or whiteboard marker that you may otherwise toss or tap. And for many people, occupying your hands with a script or speaking notes represents a further crutch necessitated more by nerves than short memory. They are often unused, and even when they are used, speakers would be more persuasive if they spoke less precisely but with greater eye contact, posture, and gesticulation.
4) *Feet*: The movement of your feet generally does more harm than good. Comfortable speakers move their feet very little, and when they do, it is with purpose. They may leave the podium to survey different parts of the room or walk forward for a more intimate

interaction with their audience. But otherwise, their feet are quiet. Avoid swaying, habitually pacing, or pointing out your hip by shifting your weight to one foot or the other. A good practice is to stand with your feet comfortably hip-width apart, with your toes pointing at your audience. It is in this position that, with good posture, you may take up space—claiming control over the room, comfortably and confidently.

5) *Mouth*: Use your mouth to smile through your nerves. Smiling puts your audience at ease. Your confidence instills their own amid the drama of live presentation. I always try to have my first sentence or two memorized and scripted. It gives me a running start. Never, under any circumstance, tell your audience that you are nervous. It is important to understand that tension or even panic inside does not typically manifest itself as obviously outside.

If you know of other ways that your nerves are expressed, be proactive. If you sweat when you present, wear dark colors. If your rate of speech picks up, write the words "Slow Down" into your notes. If you tend to stumble on words, warm up with mouth exercises in advance like a television news anchor. Ensure that you eat sufficiently before presenting to maintain your blood sugar, but don't load up on caffeine or risk a sugar spike. Ultimately, it is normal to be nervous. My old basketball coach, Ronnie Baker—who played professionally for 20 years and captained the British men's national team—once revealed that he used to vomit before every game. Before my team played in Britain's collegiate national championship, he said, "If you ain't nervous right now, you probably don't care enough." The key is to identify ways to channel your care and energy into a positive performance.

PRACTITIONER

***Spencer Boyer** is the director of the Washington office of New York University's Brennan Center for Justice. From 2012 to 2017, he served as the national intelligence officer for Europe in the National Intelligence Council, the center for long-range strategic thinking within the US intelligence community. Between August 2009 and December 2011, he served as a deputy assistant secretary of state in the Bureau of European and Eurasian Affairs. Prior to joining the State Department, Boyer was the director of international law and diplomacy at the Center for American Progress. Boyer began his professional career as an associate with the international law firm of Jones, Day, Reavis & Pogue in Washington, DC. Subsequently, he worked in The Hague as a law clerk to the president of the International Criminal Tribunal for the former Yugoslavia, in Zurich as a staff attorney at the Claims Resolution Tribunal for Dormant Accounts in Switzerland, and in Paris as counsel at the International Court of Arbitration. Boyer has also served on the Independent Task Force on US Nuclear Weapons Policy at the Council on Foreign Relations. I asked him to share his advice about preparing briefings. Here are his thoughts:*

> One of the most important lessons I have learned in my 20 years of being an international law and affairs professional is that public speaking skills—especially those geared toward addressing organizational decision makers—cannot be overestimated. Knowing how to deliver a boardroom presentation (which, for my purposes, will mean a presentation to high-level stakeholders in an institution) is a fundamental building block of professional success in numerous fields.
>
> Whether in the private, public, or nonprofit sector, a high-level briefing is often the most effective way to make an impact on senior policymakers and influence an organizational

policy process. Senior executives and officials are almost always pressed for time and thus rely on efficient, impactful presentations before making important institutional decisions. In my world, senior White House officials request and receive high-level briefings every day from across government. Ideally, an excellent presentation will lay the groundwork for well-founded policy choices. Conversely, a poor briefing can lead to misinformed or ill-informed organizational leaders who are making decisions based on incomplete or inaccurate data.

If you can give a strong briefing, you can deliver a powerful, effective set of remarks in almost any venue. Why? In essence, an excellent presentation has all the elements of any impactful public presentation: relevant subject matter, organization and timing, clarity, awareness of the audience, and passion. Fortunately, it is a skill that is entirely learnable and one that can be developed long before ever stepping into a high-level briefing.

You can develop high-level briefing skills in a number of ways, but all entail gaining experience and practice. During your time in a university, you can hone your public speaking skills through courses that require oral presentations or extracurricular activities, such as a debate, campus radio, or theater. In the work world, regular meetings where you must brief your supervisors or peers provide an opportunity to get sharper and more effective. Outside activities that require clear, concise remarks—such as being a club official and briefing on the last meeting or introducing speakers—also offer the chance to get better. In my own journey, numerous think tanks offered me opportunities to be a keynote speaker and conduct radio and television interviews on US foreign policy and national security. I focus on four primary elements in my preparation:

Subject Matter: A successful presentation has to begin with relevant, well-researched, and well-understood subject matter designed to answer a focused set of questions for your audience. When I first began giving briefings in my current areas of expertise, I needed more time to absorb the information than I do now. As you become more of an expert in your field, it becomes easier to layer on new information to your foundation. Even the most knowledgeable experts, however, need to understand fresh material well in order to give an effective presentation and potentially field queries. When it comes to a solid briefing, there is no substitute for digging deeply into a subject matter, wrestling with the content, and anticipating the tough questions.

Organization and Practice: After taking the time to research, understand, and organize your briefing material, you should practice your delivery so that the presentation is as smooth and efficient as possible. It is crucial to know the topline points with which you want your audience to come away and to design your remarks to emphasize them. "Signposts," which enable the audience to know where you are going, can be extremely helpful and prevent impatience. Even if you know your subject matter cold, if you have a disorganized presentation and do not have a few main points to emphasize, the briefing will lack impact and you may lose your listeners. The best presentations I have ever given have been ones in which I practiced my remarks more times than I thought was necessary in order to have few or no notes during delivery.

Awareness of the Audience: My first lesson in "knowing your audience" actually came 30 years ago—in my senior year of high school while running for student government. I lost my race for student body president by a few votes. I later learned that while classmates and others I personally knew voted overwhelmingly for me, I completely lost the freshman class. My victorious friend had gotten away from the podium and spoke in a targeted way that resonated with ninth-graders. My speech, by contrast, was formal and unimaginative. While it did not matter to those who already knew me, I did not pick up new supporters. I have remembered this experience throughout my career, especially in federal government, when having to present to numerous stakeholders from across agencies and outside of government. Awareness of an audience's interests, biases, concerns, and priorities can help you craft a presentation that will "speak" to them and answer their unasked questions.

Passion: Deliver your material with passion. A side benefit of doing work you love is that you will likely be drawing from material you find fascinating when developing a briefing. This fascination will come through as you speak. Show me a boring presentation, and I will show you someone who is not terribly interested in his or her work. Conversely, I would wager that professors or public speakers you still remember fondly from years ago cared deeply for the subjects about which they spoke. To the extent possible, find presentation material you care about. Your enthusiasm will show and draw others in.

PARAGON

Lawrence Lessig is a law professor and ethicist at Harvard Law School who has dedicated recent years to raising awareness about and addressing the disproportionate influence of private donors on public policy–making in the United States. A pivotal moment in his campaign was a presentation he delivered as a TED Talk in April 2013. It is part briefing, part lecture, part speech; but it combines all of the elements of good presentation style. Fewer than 18 minutes long, Lessig embeds digestible data in an odd but memorable metaphor and then pieces together a moral and practical argument that has been viewed and read by millions. While his presentation content is more rhetorical than the kind of intelligence briefing Spencer Boyer has delivered countless times to far more exclusive audiences, it features an excellent delivery that is substantive and stylish (despite utterly quirky slides). He is conscious of his audience's relatively low level of awareness about campaign finance and tailors his remarks accordingly. His message was persuasive and popular enough that he was actually emboldened to make a short-lived bid for the Democratic Party's 2016 presidential nomination. Here is the transcript of his TED Talk:

(a) TED

(b)

We the People, and the Republic We Must Reclaim
April 2013

0:11 Once upon a time, there was a place called Lesterland. Now Lesterland looks a lot like the United States. Like the United States, it has about 311 million people, and of that 311 million people, it turns out 144,000 are called Lester. If Matt's in the audience, I just borrowed that; I'll return it in a second, this character from your series. So 144,000 are called Lester, which means about .05 percent is named Lester. Now, Lesters in Lesterland have this extraordinary power. There are two elections every election cycle in Lesterland. One is called the general election. The other is called the Lester election. And in the general election, it's the citizens who get to vote, but in the Lester election, it's the Lesters who get to vote. And here's the trick. In order to run in the general election, you must do extremely well in the Lester election. You don't necessarily have to win, but you must do extremely well.

1:16 Now, what can we say about democracy in Lesterland? What we can say, number one, as the Supreme Court said in Citizens United, that people have the ultimate influence over elected officials because, after all, there is a general election, but only after the Lesters have had their way with the candidates who wish to run in the general election. And number two, obviously, this dependence upon the Lesters is going to produce a subtle, understated, we could say camouflaged, bending to keep the Lesters happy. Okay, so we have a democracy, no doubt, but it's dependent upon the Lesters and dependent upon the people. It has competing dependencies, we could say conflicting dependencies, depending upon who the Lesters are. Okay. That's Lesterland.

2:08 Now there are three things I want you to see now that I've described Lesterland. Number one, the United States is Lesterland. The United States is Lesterland. The United States also looks like this, also has two elections, one we called the general election, the second we should call the money election. In the general election, it's the citizens who get to vote, if you're over 18, in some states if you have an ID. In the money election, it's the funders who get to vote, the funders who get to vote, and just like in Lesterland, the trick is, to run in the general election, you must do extremely well in the money election. You don't necessarily have to win. There is Jerry Brown. But you must do extremely well. And here's the key: There are just as few relevant funders in USA-land as there are Lesters in Lesterland.

2:56 Now you say, really? Really .05 percent? Well, here are the numbers from 2010: .26 percent of America gave 200 dollars or more to any federal candidate, .05 percent gave the maximum amount to any federal candidate, .01 percent—the one percent of the one percent—gave $10,000 or more to federal candidates, and in this election cycle, my favorite statistic is .000042 percent—for those of you doing the numbers, you know that's 132 Americans—gave 60 percent of the Super PAC money spent in the cycle we have just seen ending. So I'm just a lawyer, I look at this range of numbers, and I say it's fair for me to say it's .05 percent who are our relevant funders in America. In this sense, the funders are our Lesters.

3:49 Now, what can we say about this democracy in USA-land? Well, as the Supreme Court said in Citizens United, we could say, of course the people have the ultimate influence over the elected officials. We have a general election, but only after the funders have had their way with the candidates who wish to run in that general election. And number two, obviously, this dependence upon the funders produces a subtle, understated, camouflaged bending to keep the funders happy. Candidates for Congress and Members of Congress spend between 30 and 70 percent of their time raising money to get back to Congress or to get their party back into power, and the question we need to ask is, what does it do to them, these humans, as they spend their time behind the telephone, calling people they've never met, but calling the tiniest slice of the one percent? As anyone would, as they do this, they develop a sixth sense, a constant awareness about how what they do might affect their ability to raise money. They become, in the words of *The X-Files*, shape-shifters, as they constantly adjust their views in light of what they know will help them to raise money, not on issues one to 10, but on issues 11 to 1,000. Leslie Byrne, a Democrat from Virginia, describes that when she went to Congress, she was told by a colleague, "Always lean to the green." Then to clarify, she went on, "He was not an environmentalist." (Laughter)

5:19 So here too we have a democracy, a democracy dependent upon the funders and dependent upon the people, competing dependencies, possibly conflicting dependencies depending upon who the funders are.

5:33 Okay, the United States is Lesterland, point number one. Here's point number two. The United States is worse than

Lesterland, worse than Lesterland because you can imagine in Lesterland if we Lesters got a letter from the government that said, "Hey, you get to pick who gets to run in the general election," we would think maybe of a kind of aristocracy of Lesters. You know, there are Lesters from every part of social society. There are rich Lesters, poor Lesters, black Lesters, white Lesters, not many women Lesters, but put that to the side for one second. We have Lesters from everywhere. We could think, "What could we do to make Lesterland better?" It's at least possible the Lesters would act for the good of Lesterland. But in our land, in this land, in USA-land, there are certainly some sweet Lesters out there, many of them in this room here today; but the vast majority of Lesters act for the Lesters because the shifting coalitions that are comprising the .05 percent are not comprising it for the public interest. It's for their private interest. In this sense, the USA is worse than Lesterland.

6:34 And finally, point number three: Whatever one wants to say about Lesterland, against the background of its history, its traditions, in our land, in USA-land, Lesterland is a corruption, a corruption. Now, by corruption I don't mean brown paper bag cash secreted among Members of Congress. I don't mean Rod Blagojevich sense of corruption. I don't mean any criminal act. The corruption I'm talking about is perfectly legal. It's a corruption relative to the framers' baseline for this republic. The framers gave us what they called a republic; but by a republic they meant a representative democracy, and by a representative democracy, they meant a government, as Madison put it in "Federalist 52," that would have a branch that would be dependent upon the people alone.

7:26 So here's the model of government. They have the people and the government with this exclusive dependency, but the problem here is that Congress has evolved a different dependence, no longer a dependence upon the people alone, increasingly a dependence upon the funders. Now this is a dependence too, but it's different and conflicting from a dependence upon the people alone so long as the funders are not the people. This is a corruption.

7:55 Now, there's good news and bad news about this corruption. One bit of good news is that it's bipartisan, equal-opportunity corruption. It blocks the left on a whole range of issues that we on the left really care about. It blocks the right too, as it makes principled arguments of the right increasingly impossible. So the right wants smaller government. When Al Gore was vice president, his team had an idea for deregulating a significant portion of the telecommunications industry. The chief policy man took this idea to Capitol Hill, and as he reported back to me, the response was, "Hell no! If we deregulate these guys, how are we going to raise money from them?"

8:34 This is a system that's designed to save the status quo, including the status quo of big and invasive government. It works against the left and the right, and that, you might say, is good news.

8:46 But here's the bad news. It's a pathological, democracy-destroying corruption, because in any system where the members are dependent upon the tiniest fraction of us for their election, that means the tiniest number of us, the tiniest, tiniest number of us, can block reform. . . .

9:13 Because there is an economy here, an economy of influence, an economy with lobbyists at the center which feeds on polarization. It feeds on dysfunction. The worse that it is for us, the better that it is for this fundraising.

9:30 Henry David Thoreau: "There are a thousand hacking at the branches of evil to one who is striking at the root." This is the root.

9:42 Okay, now, every single one of you knows this. You couldn't be here if you didn't know this, yet you ignore it. You ignore it. This is an impossible problem. You focus on the possible problems, like eradicating polio from the world or taking an image of every single street across the globe or building the first real universal translator or building a fusion factory in your garage. These are the manageable problems, so you ignore—(Laughter) (Applause)—so you ignore this corruption.

10:20 But we cannot ignore this corruption anymore. (Applause) We need a government that works. And not works for the left or the right but works for the left and the right, the citizens of the left and right, because there is no sensible reform possible until we end this corruption. So I want you to take hold, to grab the issue you care the most about. Climate change is mine, but it might be financial reform or a simpler tax system or inequality. Grab that issue, sit it down in front of you, look straight in its eyes, and tell it there is no Christmas this year. There will never be a Christmas. We will never get your issue solved until we fix this issue first. So it's not that mine is the most important issue. It's not. Yours is the most important issue, but mine is the first issue, the issue we have to solve before we get to fix the issues you care about. No sensible reform, and we cannot afford a world, a future, with no sensible reform.

11:28 Okay. So how do we do it? Turns out, the analytics here are easy, simple. If the problem is members spending an extraordinary amount of time fundraising from the tiniest slice of America, the solution is to have them spend less time fundraising but fundraise from a wider slice of Americans, to spread it out, to spread the funder influence so that we restore the idea of dependence upon the people alone. And to do this does not require a constitutional amendment, changing the First Amendment. To do this would require a single statute, a statute establishing what we think of as small dollar-funded elections, a statute of citizen-funded campaigns, and there's any number of these proposals out there: Fair Elections Now Act, the American Anti-Corruption Act, an idea in my book that I call the Grant and Franklin Project to give vouchers to people to fund elections, an idea of John Sarbanes called the

Grassroots Democracy Act. Each of these would fix this corruption by spreading out the influence of funders to all of us.

12:33 The analytics are easy here. It's the politics that's hard, indeed impossibly hard, because this reform would shrink K Street, and Capitol Hill, as Congressman Jim Cooper, a Democrat from Tennessee, put it, has become a farm league for K Street, a farm league for K Street. Members and staffers and bureaucrats have an increasingly common business model in their head, a business model focused on their life after government, their life as lobbyists. Fifty percent of the Senate between 1998 and 2004 left to become lobbyists, 42 percent of the House. Those numbers have only gone up, and as United Republic calculated last April, the average increase in salary for those who they tracked was 1,452 percent. So it's fair to ask, how is it possible for them to change this? Now I get this skepticism.

13:39 I get this cynicism. I get this sense of impossibility. But I don't buy it. This is a solvable issue. If you think about the issues our parents tried to solve in the 20th century, issues like racism or sexism or the issue that we've been fighting in this century, homophobia, those are hard issues. You don't wake up one day no longer a racist. It takes generations to tear that intuition, that DNA, out of the soul of a people. But this is a problem of just incentives, just incentives. Change the incentives, and the behavior changes; and the states that have adopted small dollar–funded systems have seen overnight a change in the practice. When Connecticut adopted this system, in the very first year, 78 percent of elected representatives gave up large contributions and took small contributions only. It's solvable, not by being a Democrat, not by being a Republican. It's solvable by being citizens, by being citizens, by being TEDizens. Because if you want to kickstart reform, look, I could kickstart reform at half the price of fixing energy policy, I could give you back a republic.

15:03 Okay. But even if you're not yet with me, even if you believe this is impossible, what the five years since I spoke at TED has taught me as I've spoken about this issue again and again is, even if you think it's impossible, that is irrelevant. Irrelevant. I spoke at Dartmouth once, and a woman stood up after I spoke, I write in my book, and she said to me, "Professor, you've convinced me this is hopeless. Hopeless. There's nothing we can do." When she said that, I scrambled. I tried to think, "How do I respond to that hopelessness? What is that sense of hopelessness?" And what hit me was an image of my six-year-old son. And I imagined a doctor coming to me and saying, "Your son has terminal brain cancer, and there's nothing you can do. Nothing you can do." So would I do nothing? Would I just sit there? Accept it? Okay, nothing I can do? I'm going off to build Google Glass. Of course not. I would do everything I could, and I would do everything I could because this is what love means, that the odds are irrelevant and that you do whatever the hell you can, the odds be damned. And then I saw the obvious link, because even we liberals love this country.

16:31 And so when the pundits and the politicians say that change is impossible, what this love of country says back is, "That's just irrelevant." We lose something dear, something everyone in this room loves and cherishes, if we lose this republic, and so we act with everything we can to prove these pundits wrong.

16:55 So here's my question: Do you have that love? Do you have that love? Because if you do, then what the hell are you, what are the hell are we doing?

17:12 When Ben Franklin was carried from the Constitutional Convention in September of 1787, he was stopped in the street by a woman who said, "Mr. Franklin, what have you wrought?" Franklin said, "A republic, madam, if you can keep it." A republic. A representative democracy. A government dependent upon the people alone. We have lost that republic. All of us have to act to get it back.

17:53 Thank you very much.

https://www.ted.com/talks/lawrence_lessig_we_the_people_and_the_republic_we_must_reclaim/transcript?language=en

6

THE BROADCAST APPEARANCE

PRINCIPLES

Reaching the General Public

Broadcast appearances bring the fundamentals of a briefing to a studio setting with an even more demanding, but unseen, audience. These appearances are interviews and commentary that you are invited to provide by podcast, radio, or television broadcast networks. They are typically unsolicited by you. Instead, a guest booker—a producer who is responsible for curating on-air participation by relevant experts, witnesses, or newsmakers—will contact you. However, larger organizations may have a publicity office that makes your availability known to guest bookers, should there be a reason to invite you on a show. These appearances are normally unpaid in North America, but honoraria are offered elsewhere.

Most live television and radio interviews last between 2 and 8 minutes, and producers prefer answers that are under 30 seconds. If your interview is recorded, it will likely be edited down to select sound bites that last anywhere from 3 to 15 seconds. The vogue in radio and television today entails quick cuts and short clips. Consequently, there is an increasing premium on—yet again—brevity. The key is to make compelling arguments or statements in a very short time span. However, it is not as simple as repurposing the pithy summary statements and topic sentences from your executive summary or the lead from your op-ed or press release. Text is but one aspect of the appearance. Television, radio, and podcasts incorporate multiple dimensions of communication at once. As with printed text, the heart of your ideas will be the words you choose. With radio and podcasts, these words are enhanced by the tone you invoke. With broadcast appearances—like briefings—the text and sound are further enhanced by your image and your nonverbal communication from hand gestures, facial expressions, and posture.

However, unlike briefings, your words—called a voiceover, or "V.O."—plug into supporting video and photography that is occasionally played over them by producers. So merely repurposing the pithy statements from your executive summary without considering how other dimensions of communication may enrich its message is missing an opportunity to engage your viewers. You are also likely to be ineffective. Television viewers and radio listeners have come to expect information to be accompanied by action, emotion, and amusement—in short, entertainment—in a very short period of time. Should you fail to deliver, you risk losing their attention.

This fickle nature is reflective of a viewership that is not truly invested in your subject matter or may have other things going on in their individual lives. The television or streaming content may be playing while they wash dishes. This is why, quite separately from briefings, part of your challenge is to persuade your audience that your issue and ideas are worth their time—that they should stay tuned. The good news is that getting on television is half the battle. Broadcast companies are trained judges of what engages their audience, so if you are welcomed onto a show, it is likely because there is an expectation that the audience will find the subject matter interesting. The other half of the battle is persuading these viewers that you are a credible source with an opinion or perspective that merits support. With all its vividness, color, and slickness, broadcast appearances therefore represent an enormous opportunity to spread your ideas widely.

In *Words That Work*, Frank Luntz wrote that the key to successful language for products or politics is "to personalize and humanize the message to trigger an emotional remembrance. As Warren Beatty, perhaps the best student of the human condition in Hollywood, once told me," he wrote, "people will forget what you say, but they will never forget how you made them feel." He continues, "If the listener can apply the language to a general situation or human condition, you have achieved *humanization*. But if the listener can relate the language to his or her own life experiences, that's *personalization*."[1]

Adapted for the Screen

The advantage of broadcast interviews is that the style is conversational. The best respondents are those who can maintain the casual ease of a friendly discussion but offer substantial ideas under bright lights and in front of a camera (or three). The particulars of broadcast appearances warrant adapting a

1. Luntz, F. (2007). *Words that work: It's not what you say, it's what people hear*. New York, NY: Hachette Books, 18.

few of the fundamentals of oral communication addressed in the preceding chapter:

Eye Contact: Interviews for television usually take place in one of three formats: you are interviewed in a studio with the anchor, on-site (such as in your office or in front of a news setting), or through a remote format where you and the anchor are in different studios. When you are interviewed on-site or in a studio with an anchor, it is conventional to maintain eye contact with the interviewer, as you would in a typical off-camera discussion. Remote interviews, in contrast, pose a greater challenge. To make eye contact, you will need to stare directly into a camera lens, responding to the anchor's prompts as heard through an earpiece. Today, many such cameras are remotely controlled, so there may not even be a technician in the studio with you. Having a conversation without another human present feels extremely unnatural. However, it is even more awkward to watch an interview with a guest whose eyes are wandering and not looking into the camera! So it is worth practicing looking at an inanimate object while having a conversation or presenting an argument before your first remote television experience.

Tone Variation: Television—but also radio—can easily turn into background noise. And unlike briefings, your audience is not captive; television viewers and radio listeners can change the station. On television and especially during radio interviews, varying the tone of your statements to match their content is essential to maintain viewer interest. Tone is the primary way to communicate the sarcasm, seriousness, pity, levity, and force that enhance the content of our statements. This does not require shouting, shrieking, sighing, or other overt and extreme changes in tone; rather, it requires the same variation each of us expects in cordial dialogue in more conventional circumstances.

Gestures: Gestures are a helpful way to complement the enhancement provided by variations in tone on television. On-camera gestures need to be simple and strategic. The typical camera frame captures merely the area above your sternum—the center of your chest—and only a few inches wider than your shoulders. So any gesture that is not directly in front of your chest is unlikely to even appear on screen. Overly lively gestures can distract viewers from the content of your statements, rather than enhance their meaning or force. Naturally, on radio, anything otherwise visible must be transferred to changes in tone and description.

Rate: Because broadcast appearances tend to be so brief, respondents may feel pressure to speak quickly to cram in their ideas. Remember: television is not the medium for comprehensiveness; it is the medium for brevity. So those who speak too quickly tend to be those who have not invested enough effort in distilling their ideas into pithy, punchy statements that summarize more complicated positions in an engaging way.

Two challenges arise. First, networks increasingly crave conflict and controversy in debate settings, making for a more hostile dynamic on the air. Some invited guests believe that power is commanded by the person who controls the microphone, and this leads to seemingly endless blathering as a means of preventing a counterpart from speaking. However, unconstrained emotion and rambling dilute the credibility and power of your perspective. It suggests a lack of focus, and it is usually unappealing for viewers. (If you are ever on the receiving end of this, attempt to assert yourself forcefully but resist exhibiting frustration. Viewers will see you take the high road and find you more persuasive.) Manage your rate to demonstrate your command.

In debate settings, the reporter or anchor will usually ensure that both interviewees have an opportunity to make an opening remark. After the openings, it may turn into a free-for-all. If the reporter or anchor does not balance the air time, you may need to assert yourself into a pause left by your counterpart or risk not speaking at all.

In other circumstances, a broadcast network may invite you to speak as an expert alongside a reporter or alongside one or two more politically motivated counterparts. In this role, you are there to serve as a reference point. It is important to speak authoritatively and contrast your counterparts' journalism, emotion, or advocacy with well-substantiated commentary and objective analysis that places current events in perspective. In this format, you are not competing with your counterparts for airtime but instead complementing their statements. Again, manage your rate to demonstrate your command.

As a dispassionate but knowledgeable party, your goal is to inform the impressions of your audience and shape the conclusions they draw from the news segment. While you should address your on-air counterparts directly, remember that your ultimate goal lies with those on the other side of the camera.

Second, during personal interviews, reporters and anchors often ask three or four questions at once. ("Professor Gest, how did we get here? People want to know why this is happening. What can we do about it?") This may lead you to feel pressure to answer all questions and cause you to hurry your rate and lose your form. A better strategy is to maintain good pace and view this as an opportunity. Simply address the most fundamental question, the question for which you are best prepared, or the question about which you feel most strongly. If this leaves the correspondent dissatisfied, rest assured she or he will follow up with whatever question is outstanding. Asking a barrage of questions is poor form by the reporter or anchor, who should know that once you ask more than one question, you permit the respondent to digress, evade, and more subtly direct the interview in the manner he or she prefers. (Remember this if the tables ever turn and you are the questioner.)

Dress: As with any other live presentation that you are giving as an expert, analyst, or official, ensure that you dress the part. In the way that handwriting can matter when you write a school exam, however unfairly, your appearance matters when you present your ideas. If you appear to take your presentation seriously, you will be perceived as someone who should be taken seriously. This is particularly true if you appear under 40 years old and are likely to be underestimated. Do not worry about being "overdressed," even on a Sunday interview. The anchor will likely be wearing a suit and, if the anchor is a man, a necktie. Furthermore, television studios are notoriously cold thanks to aggressive air conditioning. (Anchors wear a substantial amount of makeup on the air, and sweat looks bad.) You'll be happy to wear a blazer and slacks, or a professional blouse and skirt or business-like dress. Psychology researchers show that inferences of competence based solely on facial appearance predicted the outcomes of US congressional elections better than chance (e.g., 68.8 percent of the Senate races in 2004) and were related to the margin of victory. These findings suggest that snap judgments about appearance can contribute to choices that are widely assumed to be based on rational and deliberative consideration.[2]

Frames: When you are on the air, and particularly when you are in the company of those who are attempting to discount or dispute your ideas, you should ensure that you frame your thoughts on your terms and not those of the opposition. In *The Political Mind*, Lakoff shows why this is so important: "When I teach frame semantics, I give my class a task: Don't think of an elephant! The point is that you can't do it. The reason is

2. Willis, J., & Todorov, A. (2006). First impressions: Making up your mind after a 100-ms exposure to a face. *Psychological Science*, *17*(7), 592–598.

that words are defined in terms of frames, and when used, the words activate those frames, whether negated or not. This is important for people in politics to know. If you use the opposition's frames, even to negate or argue against them, you are helping them because you are activating their frames in the minds of the public, and their frames in turn activate their worldview."[3] Consider your terms of reference well in advance, and incorporate them in your everyday speech so that by the time you are on the air, your expression of them is natural. Staying within your frames may entail repetition in order to return the discussion to your terms and reinforce your message to viewers and listeners. In fact, repetition promotes the retention of information and can suggest confidence in the assertions made, but there must be a balance with supportive content. Too much repetition makes the speaker appear robotic, shallow, cautious, and therefore untrustworthy.

Make Yourself Comfortable

Television and radio can induce angst and nervousness. You know that thousands, possibly millions, of people (whom you cannot see) are watching and listening to you, and this increases our perception of the magnitude of our actions.[4]

3. Lakoff, George (2008). *The political mind: Why you can't understand 21st-century politics with an 18th-century brain*. New York, NY: Penguin.

4. Steinmetz, J., Xu, Q., Fishbach, A., & Zhang, Y. (2016). Being observed magnifies action. *Journal of Personality and Social Psychology*, *111*(6), 852–865. Retrieved from http://dx.doi.org/10.1037/pspi0000065

The camera seems to exaggerate your movements in its zoomed-in frame that records your statements in perpetuity. However, there are a number of helpful steps you can take to make yourself more comfortable.

First, if the purpose of the interview or appearance is to share expertise, it is reasonable to request the questions you will be asked in advance. If the producer will not share questions or is uncertain of them, it is reasonable to request the thematic areas the anchor or reporter will want to cover. This is in everyone's best interest. You will communicate more effectively and be more at ease if you are able to prepare for and anticipate questions—particularly in the case of a live interview. The producer, reporter, and network prefer that the people they select to interview for expertise sound like experts and provide interesting, germane answers. The viewers will prefer that the interviewee not require constant clarification or not know the answer to a number of questions. Use this interaction with the producer to also ensure that they spell and pronounce your name, title, and affiliation correctly.

However, note that this does not hold if the purpose of your interview is to debate a subject matter with another guest or if you are running for office or represent an elected official or agency. The purpose—and therefore the nature—of the interview then changes. The interview is a test of your knowledge, character, or viewpoints. That does not mean you can't request the questions in advance; at a minimum, you should ask for the name of the anchor and the show on which you will appear. Requests from government officials or candidates, however, may lead producers to be more guarded and less forthcoming on details. In such cases, the unexpected makes for better television and radio and a better test of your capacity for quick thinking in your responses.

Second, to better prepare yourself for the show on which you will appear, always watch or listen to clips from the network's website or YouTube page. This is advisable not only to accustom yourself to the style and personalities of the anchors and the nature of the show but also to make sure that this is a program with which you want to be associated—that the show's agenda is not incompatible with your purposes. This does not mean that you should avoid addressing audiences that are inclined to disagree with you. Rather, you should be wary if a show is amateurish, has a reputation for disinformation, or will attempt to employ your comments to advance its agenda.

I once agreed to an interview on RT—a Russian government–backed international news network. The anchor's principal objective was to disparage the United States with baseless assertions and conspiracies, and he attempted to twist my commentary to fit his worldview. I am not a blind nationalist, but I am also not interested in participating in overt propaganda. In hindsight, it was a mistake to agree to the interview. There was hardly any opportunity to provide a counternarrative to what the anchor said.

Third, prepare remarks, but do not feel too much pressure to entertain your audience with humor. Even if you have been invited onto a late night or comedy talk show, you will not be expected to make people laugh if that is not reflective of your normal style. Comedy shows rely on experts to contrast with and set up the comedian's jokes; news broadcasts entertain with drama and gravity.

The most useful steps you can take are to prepackage a few sound bites in advance to address expected questions. Sound bites are assertive, punchy, even memorable statements that encompass broader points. They may play on words and use metaphors, similes, or analogies that invigorate the subject matter in a memorable, engaging manner. At the same time, just because you have prepared a sound bite that may sound clever in isolation does not mean that you must use it on the show. If a natural opportunity to use it does not present itself, you are better off following the flow of conversation. Injecting a sound bite for a sound bite's sake will appear forced and scripted.

Fourth, remember that viewers of live television expect less polish, and they forgive errors. Many people who find live interviews frightening or intimidating are fixated on the fact that there are no rehearsals, edits, or second takes. It seems like there is very little room for error. However, this is an unhelpful way to conceive of live television. Viewers do not expect TV interviews to sound like slickly edited movies. Even in rehearsed interviews, it is expected that speech will contain flaws. And when you stumble or mispronounce a word, keep rolling the way you would in any other conversation. Once you move on, the audience will too. The best thing you can do? Relax.

PRACTITIONERS

Lyndsay Duncombe and Bill Schneider are both television professionals. While Ms. Duncombe has a background in production as a reporter for the Canadian Broadcasting Corporation (CBC), Dr. Schneider turned his academic expertise into a career as a top political analyst for CNN. Given their different perspectives on broadcast appearances, I asked them to contribute advice separately.

Lyndsay Duncombe *is a journalist and senior editor for the CBC's Washington Bureau, responsible for coordinating* *coverage of US politics for all CBC platforms. She also provides live reports and analysis on CBC NewsNetwork, CBC Radio One, and* The National. *She has reported on the 2016 and 2020 US presidential elections across many US states. Her previous postings include Los Angeles, Manitoba, and Saskatchewan.*

The challenge with communicating on live television is that you have to be natural in an unnatural situation. To look past the lights in your eyes and think past the cues in your ear and engage your audience. The goal is to come across as though you are having a real conversation with a human being, instead of yammering into a dark camera lens. Some people are naturally good at this, but anyone can get better with practice.

I started doing live reports on local news in Winnipeg, Manitoba. There are no cameras in courtrooms in Canada. So I would often run out and explain the details of a complicated criminal verdict moments after it was delivered. I reported from crime scenes in frigid weather, counted mosquitoes in mosquito traps, and interviewed children, hockey players, and cabinet ministers—all live. What I learned doing that has prepared me to report from the White House lawn and at breaking news stories across the United States.

Focus is key. One of the real dangers of live TV is rambling off-topic. If you have a brief television spot or interview, take a few moments to narrow what you want to say into key phrases or points. Writing them down helps. Saying them out loud is even better. When I'm about to go on television, I'll often practice with my cameraman. He finds it a bit annoying, but it helps. Practicing out loud allows you to edit things that don't make sense. After you run through what you want to say a few times, you become more concise and conversational.

Try to avoid insider words. One of my best friends is a cancer scientist. She often gets media requests about her studies, so she'll call me and go over what she plans to say. Inevitably, she will be eloquent and passionate but use words only people who are trying to cure cancer understand. So I ask her to explain again, like she would if we were sitting down and having a glass of wine and she was telling me about her day. Choosing simpler words doesn't assume your audience is less intelligent or informed than you; they could be intelligent and informed in different areas. Another way to think about it is to speak as though you were explaining your work to someone you met on a plane. You have no idea what they know or what they don't, so you use everyday language to delve into complicated subjects.

Roll with the unexpected. Weird things happen on live TV, and the best thing to do is just to acknowledge it. If you let the audience in on what is going on, they will be forgiving. If you pretend all is okay when it's not, it can look awkward. I made this mistake in Indiana recently.

Senator Ted Cruz was about to drop out of the race for the 2016 Republican presidential nomination. But there was far bigger news in Canada: 80,000 people were being evacuated from the city of Fort MacMurray because of a forest fire. I was standing by for the better part of an hour, unsure when or if they would come to me for the story about Cruz. The moment they finally did was chaotic. Just as I started talking on-air, an aggressive and grouchy still photographer tried to barrel his way through our shot. Instead of letting him pass, my cameraman tried to stop him. They were having a mime-like fight in my peripheral vision, just as Cruz is breaking news and I'm trying to sound intelligent. My best bet would have been to say, "Let's let this guy pass. It's crowded in here" and then moved on. Instead, I looked distracted, and the audience had no idea why.

Everyone worries about how they look on TV, and almost everyone hates how they look on TV. You will probably hate how you look on TV, but the audience won't be as critical. When you are thinking about what to wear or how to present yourself, the biggest thing to remember is not to be distracting.

Your outfit and appearance shouldn't draw attention away from your content. As a general rule, that means avoiding crazy prints, exotic hairstyles, and sparkling bling, unless that's how you typically dress, because the biggest thing that resonates on television is being genuine. When a message is shared with authenticity and enthusiasm, it gets noticed and remembered.

***Bill Schneider** is a contributor to* The Hill. *From 1990 to 2009, he was CNN's senior political analyst. He has covered every US presidential and midterm election since 1976 for the* Los Angeles Times, The Atlantic, *CNN, and Al Jazeera. He has also covered elections in other countries, including the United Kingdom, Germany, Mexico, Israel, and Japan. He was a member of the CNN political team that won an Emmy for its 2006 election coverage and a Peabody Award for its 2008 coverage.*

As a columnist for 30 years, I learned quickly that anything you have to say can be said in 750 words. It had better be, because your editor will reduce it to that length. On television, you learn very quickly that you'd better be able to make your point in twenty seconds or less. Because your producer will tell you to "wrap."

Many years ago, when I was still freelancing, I got a call from a booker for a well-known late-night television news program asking me to comment on an issue I really didn't know much about. I gave her the name of a renowned academic expert on the subject. When I watched the show that night, I saw that they had booked someone of far less reputation. The next day, I asked the booker if she had reached the person I recommended. Yes, she replied, but she decided not to use him. "Why not?"" I asked. "Well," she said, "we found him rather thoughtful." Thoughtful? What could that mean? It meant that he prefaced his answers by saying, "There are four reasons why this is happening." Four reasons? That will never do on television. Your producer will tell you, "Pick one."

An analyst is an explainer: "Here's what happened today, and this is what it means." He appears on news broadcasts, usually alone, to offer context and interpretation. Can an analyst express an opinion? Sure. But he has to be able to back his assertions with evidence, albeit not too much evidence. This is television, after all, not an academic seminar. But he has to convince viewers that he can defend what he is saying. An analyst must communicate authority. Viewers have to trust him.

My baptism under fire in television news came during the Clarence Thomas confirmation hearings in 1991. When the committee hearings reconvened to consider Anita Hill's sensational testimony, I was put on the air to provide a running analysis of what it all meant. There was only one problem: no one knew what it all meant, especially members of the Senate Judiciary Committee.

I figured out that the Republican strategy was to turn the hearings into a trial. In a trial, the burden of proof is on the accuser. Hill would have to prove that Thomas had harassed her. The issue would become her credibility, not his. No one could personally corroborate Anita Hill's story that Thomas had sexually harassed her. And no one could personally corroborate Thomas's story that he had never done so. Witnesses who claimed that Thomas harassed other women or that Hill fantasized about her relationships with men were found to have little credibility. Only two things were established—that it was "out of character" for Hill to lie and that it was "out of character" for Thomas to harass women.

I tried to explain to the viewing audience that a confirmation hearing is not a trial, to no apparent effect. During the Senate debate, most speakers focused on one issue: who was telling the truth, Thomas or Hill? Only a few senators bothered to address the real issues: Thomas's constitutional philosophy, his judicial experience, and his legal qualifications.

The notion of a person's being innocent until proven guilty is deeply ingrained in American culture. Refusing to confirm Thomas became tantamount to declaring him guilty of an unproven charge. To the American public, that seemed unfair. American audiences "get" trials. They had watched *Perry Mason* for years. Turning the confirmation hearings into a trial was a perfect strategy for deflecting attention away from the real issue—whether Thomas was qualified to serve on the nation's highest court.

That, more or less, is what you do as a political analyst. You figure things out. You explain what's going on. The skills required are those of a communicator: clarity and conciseness. As it happens, those are the same skills required of a good teacher. Having something interesting to say is essential. Being able to communicate it effectively is equally important.

PARAGON

Neil deGrasse Tyson is the Frederick P. Rose Director and Head of the Hayden Planetarium in New York City and a research associate of the Department of Astrophysics at the American Museum of Natural History. He holds a PhD in astrophysics from Columbia University, and his research interests include star formation, exploding stars, dwarf galaxies, and the structure of the Milky Way. He is an expert with bona fide scientific credentials and many academic publications. However, he has found a calling in translating some of the most complicated concepts in the physical sciences to broad audiences and readers. Tyson has authored or coauthored 13 popular books, and, from 1995 to 2005 he was a monthly essayist for Natural History *magazine. He has also served as an editor or on-camera host of several television programs and podcasts. In this example, he is interviewed by CNN anchor Fareed Zakaria, a highly qualified "translator" himself.*

Fareed Zakaria is a dynamic journalist and political commentator who—like Tyson—received first-class academic training, which he translated into a career in the news media. A polymath with a particular interest in international relations, Zakaria has written numerous books and hundreds of in-depth articles. However, more commonly, he is asked to condense these ideas into sound bytes for his television program, Fareed Zakaria GPS, *and his appearances on other CNN broadcasts. Often, he converts content directly from his opinion column in* The Washington Post. *Each time he does so, he is challenged to consolidate and simplify his consideration of a subject into a brief broadcast segment.*

Zakaria has a particular gift for reducing complex debates into simple opposing arguments and succinct questions, which he lobs at Tyson. Zakaria also regularly makes use of pauses and rhetorical questions, as if he is having a conversation with himself. For his part, Tyson employs a clever, relatable metaphor that likens the universe's fundamental elements to baking ingredients to help his audience understand the way that humans are derived from the cosmos and the strong likelihood of extraterrestrial life. He also speaks in a jovial, conversational manner that you would sooner expect to hear on someone's back porch, but it is precisely the simplicity of his language, his gesticulations, and his informality that make him so approachable.

(a) CNN

(b)

May 8, 2017

Fareed Zakaria GPS: “A Science Lesson with Neil deGrasse Tyson“

ZAKARIA: Do you ever look up at the myriad stars on a clear night and wonder how they got here? Ever wonder how big the universe really is or how it all began? Well, wonder no more. My next guest is probably the world's most famous and favorite scientist. Neil deGrasse Tyson has a new book out called *Astrophysics for People in a Hurry*. This is great for us because television is always in a hurry. Neil, welcome back to the show.

TYSON: Thanks, Fareed, always good to be on your show.

ZAKARIA: So you begin with the Big Bang. You actually begin before the Big Bang.

TYSON: Yeah, the name of the first chapter is “In the Beginning,” so . . . (laughter) . . . when else would you begin such a story? That's right. The Big Bang is the first sentence. It just takes you there.

ZAKARIA: What I'm struck by is that the Big Bang really also is the beginning of physics, chemistry, and biology, in the way you explain it. So . . .

TYSON: Yeah.

ZAKARIA: . . . first what happens is you have this tiny, tiny dot, as it were, and it explodes.

TYSON: Yes.

ZAKARIA: Right? And out of that, explain what happens?

TYSON: Yeah, so, there's still some unknown elements of this chapter, very earliest chapter in the history of the universe. But what's intriguing is the—how, as the universe expands, certain laws of physics take shape and other laws of physics begin to manifest. And so some of the great challenges of early-universe cosmologists is untangling what happened when. And so—and this allows you to imagine other universes—this is where the concept of a multi-verse comes in—other universes where the laws of physics took a slightly different turn earlier in the universe and you get a whole other kind of bubble, some other kind of—somebody else's Big Bang that may have laws of physics that might not be favorable to life itself.

ZAKARIA: So you also talk about, in the Big Bang, how it, sort of, is the beginning of chemistry in a way. Because these particles start to interact with one another. And I've always thought that you make a very good case for people to understand how interesting chemistry is. Chemistry is often the place where you lose people in science, right? It's organic chemistry that just seems too hard. So . . .

TYSON: I love me some chemistry. And so you get chemistry when you have atoms. Because atoms come together to make, of course, molecules. But before you have an atom, you have to make the particles that make the atom. So you've got to back up to get those particles, the quarks, then the protons, neutrons, electrons. You've got to make those first. Then they come together and you make your base ingredients, hydrogen and helium. Then stars pick up the mantle.

And so I give—I give a whole chapter in there to the periodic table of elements, something I think should be one of the greatest icons of our culture. Because, think about it, when I think of a kitchen, and you want to bake a cake, you need the ingredients, the flour, the sugar, the—you want to bake the universe, or stuff in the universe, start with your ingredients.

The periodic table has the 92 elements, hydrogen through uranium, out of which everything is made.

ZAKARIA: Out of the Big Bang, the next stage, as you say, comes biology, because those chemical interactions somehow produce something that we now call life?

TYSON: Exactly. So biology is the most complex form of chemistry we know. And it's there, but here's the catch. In a separate chapter, titled "On Earth as It Is in the Heavens," the chemistry and physics on earth repeats everywhere in the universe. These elements are on the moon, on the sun, on other galaxies. And so we're not made of special ingredients. We're made of the same ingredients. To some people that's depressing, but to me that's enlightening. You're the same as the universe.

ZAKARIA: And do you think there's life outside of Earth?

TYSON: Once you look at the numbers, and the carbon—we're carbon-based life, because you can make tremendously complex molecules stringing together carbon atoms, such as our DNA—carbon is everywhere in the universe. And you look at the latest planet tally, we're rising through 3,000 planets nearby relative to the size of the galaxy. The universe has been around for 13 billion years.

Once you look at these numbers, there's no excuse thinking that we're the only life on Earth. That would be some ego talking, if that's how you said it. It's—anyone who's studied the problem recognizes the very high likelihood it would be somewhere—though we haven't found it yet, but we've got the top people working on it.

ZAKARIA: Why do you think we don't—we don't teach science well enough to hold people's attention?

TYSON: You know, that's a great question. I think science, as well as many other subjects in school, K–12, let's take, is—I think we've been—we're thinking that children are empty vessels and you unzip the head, pour in the knowledge, zip it back up, slap a diploma on them, and send them off, and then they're declared to be educated. And somewhere we're missing, as a minimum, a course not on chemistry, biology, physics, or geology but a course on what science is as an enterprise and how and why it works and how it drives curiosity and inquiry. Have that as a minimum, but on top of that teach things like analysis and interpretation and how to—to coalesce bits and pieces of information into new coherent ideas.

Then, when you come out and you're declared a graduate and some new information rises up, you don't say, "Oh, I didn't know that was true." You would say, "Let me find out whether or not that is true." And then you become a lifelong learner.

ZAKARIA: So when we look at something like global warming, how should we think about it? There are people who say, "Look, of course it's just a theory. All of science is a theory. These are hypotheses, and, you know, we should be looking at evidence." There are the scientists who say "No, no, no; it is at this point a fact."

TYSON: If anyone utters the words "It's just a theory," it means they're missing a piece of their education where they do not fully understand what science is and how and why it works. So I try not to beat folks over the head, in power, because they're duly elected by a population that wants their leadership to serve them. And I recognize that. That's the system we've all bought into.

So as an educator I look at the electorate and I say, "If you're going to make an informed decision, not only about the country's future but especially about your own future, it would be greatly enhanced by just learning how knowledge is acquired and how it is affirmed in the scientific arena."

And today you have people who—who will just accept what anyone tells them or think that they can deny an objectively established scientific truth and then—I don't mind that; in a free country, think what you want. But if you now rise to power and have—and have jurisdiction over legislation and you pivot that on what you don't know about how the world works, that's a recipe for disaster. I would say it's the beginning of the unraveling of an informed democracy.

ZAKARIA: We are always lucky to have you on.

TYSON: Fareed, always good to be here.

ZAKARIA: *Astrophysics for People in a Hurry*, Neil deGrasse Tyson.

TYSON: Thank you.

ZAKARIA: A pleasure. Next on *GPS*, you are looking at what one senior diplomat called "a gigantic failure of international diplomacy." What is it and where? We'll tell you when we come back.

LINK TO VIDEO: https://www.cnn.com/videos/tv/2017/05/08/exp-gps-0507-neil-degrasse-tyson-astrophysics.cnn

THE ELEVATOR PITCH

PRINCIPLES

Reaching the Decision Maker

An elevator pitch (or elevator speech) is required when you have a fleeting opportunity to share your ideas informally—such as when you are alone with a decision maker in an elevator for the short time it takes to get from the top floor to the lobby. Elevator pitches can take place in a chance encounter at a bar or during the walk from a Senate office building to the chamber. These are circumstances pressurized not only by time but also by the challenge of competing with distractions like incoming text messages or other people's elevator pitches. Gravity must be conveyed with brevity.

The elevator pitch combines the pithiness of a tweet with the delivery of a television interview, with the added challenge that it must be delivered with the charm expected in dialogue and an informal environment. Indeed, the elevator pitch is not a "speech" at all. The audience is not captive or necessarily acquiescent. Rather, the targeted individual may be impatient or downright uncomfortable.

There is an old debate about the relative importance between "substance" and "style"—between the strength of your ideas and how well you express them. So far, this book has been based on the premise that this is a false dichotomy. Ultimately, if your ideas are not meritorious, then effective communication merely postpones their inevitable failure. Stylish presentation is not a replacement for careful consideration, rigorous research, or calculated analysis. Equally so, and inversely, the merit of your ideas will likely remain unknown without effective communication skills. Occasionally, ideas are so powerful that they proliferate anyway, but their reach and persuasion will not achieve their full potential. There is a graveyard of brilliant arguments from the worlds of academic research and policy analysis that never make it into public consciousness. Society is subsequently worse off because of our inability, at times, to communicate.

By improving your ability to deliver elevator pitches, you acknowledge a further false dichotomy in the world of policy ideas—the relative importance of "who you know" and "what you know." Elevator pitches are sometimes anticipated but always spontaneous interactions with a decision maker who is otherwise too busy or inaccessible to listen to a full presentation or read a full memo. Feeling the need to make your pitch to such a person implies the limitations of a meritocracy in which a good idea ("what you know") eventually works its way to decision makers' desks and consciousness. The elevator pitch replaces the intermediary steps and allows you to bring the idea directly to the decision maker.

It is helpful to think of elevator pitches as containing three basic components that address three questions with three corresponding answers: Who are *you*? What do *you* want from *me*? What are the next steps for *us*?

Who Are *You*?

In my first meeting with Joshua Hoyt, a fiery Chicago organizer who just retired from leading the National Partnership for New Americans, he said, "I don't talk to no one no one sent." Admittedly, at first, I was as confused by the grammar of this statement as I was by its meaning. Josh was passing forward a long Chicago political tradition of distrust of outsiders. He was wary of anyone who showed up in his office without a referral by someone with whom he had a preexisting relationship. This tradition is not unique to Chicago. In the world of policy and advocacy, partisan alignments place a premium on loyalty. A shared connection makes you both accountable and trustworthy.

Consequently, in politics, once people move past courtesies, they will quickly want to know who you are or who recommended that you contact them. In elevator pitches, there is little time for courtesy, so it is often best to start with the magic words that open the gates to serious consideration. Some examples:

I work for Senator Gillibrand.

Keisha Jamison suggested I reach out.

You may recall we met at the RNC fundraiser last month.

John Garcia said I would find you here.

I am a friend of Amar Abbas.

But sometimes there is more than one degree of separation, and you can only offer context and try to establish a sense of legitimacy:

> I am a political scientist at George Mason University.
>
> I work in Research and Development on the ninth floor.
>
> I read your op-ed in the *Post* last week.
>
> I am an urban planning consultant at Meyers & Morehouse.
>
> I analyze poverty data at the Urban Institute.

In other circumstances, the busy decision maker may be your direct boss, and such an introduction is not necessary. In any case, leave a moment after your introduction for her reaction. She may reminisce about her time with Keisha when they were in university together or discuss her respect for Senator Gillibrand. He may mention that he just attended a conference at George Mason University or lament that his op-ed has led to a lot of complaints. Indeed, their reaction may provide a relevant detail that you can use strategically later in the pitch.

In any case, a connection and possibly a rapport can be built even if a degree or two of separation exists at the onset of the elevator pitch.

What Do *You* Want from *Me*?

Once you have cleared the initial hurdle and gotten the decision maker's attention, it is time to deftly get to the point. What are you trying to achieve? What are you trying to persuade me to believe? What are you asking me to do? The best way to frame this orientation is by finding common ground:

> I understand you are trying to defeat the proposed amendment on HR 202.
>
> We have a mutual interest in protecting the Mojave Wildlife Preserve.
>
> I recently undertook an evaluation of your public housing program.
>
> Your county will soon need to reevaluate water usage.
>
> I have followed your pro bono work on behalf of refugees from West Africa.

Each of these statements suggests that you want what the executive wants—that your interests align. In other circumstances, part of your challenge is to persuade the decision maker that something is in her or his interest:

> I want to bring your attention to unsanitary conditions in the city's orphanage.
>
> There is evidence that the new Metro station would be better placed two blocks away.
>
> I am hoping to form a partnership to address the bullying of gay high school students.
>
> Have you considered including a Bangladeshi delegation at your upcoming summit?
>
> I wanted to share the main conclusions from my memo on human trafficking.

It is at this juncture that you make your proposal, your "ask," or provide a summary of your ideas—always in the form of a well-constructed topic sentence followed by an opportunity for the decision maker to react. Reactions may vary, but a powerful, clear, succinct statement usually produces good results.

Often, the brevity of a topic sentence inspires follow-up questions. They indicate that the decision maker is choosing to extend your interaction. You are no longer intervening—you've conquered the greatest obstacle to action. Your next statements should be additional topic sentences that reveal the scope of your ideas and beg more detail.

Sometimes, the decision maker may completely disagree with you or be more subtly disinclined to support you. This is also valuable. You will not invest any further time in soliciting his support or engagement and can turn to other people or organizations. It is a tribute to the clarity of your expression that the decision maker feels comfortable enough to confidently say "no." It is also valuable because the decision maker may tell you why he or she disagrees, which will allow you to hone your message and follow up or use the lesson for the next decision maker you approach on the same topic.

And frequently, protective of her or his time, the decision maker may ask that you follow up by arranging a more formal meeting, send the specifics in an email, or contact her or his support staff. This leads directly to the third component of a successful elevator pitch.

What Are the Next Steps Between *Us*?

Conclude your elevator pitch with the acknowledgment of a concrete next step in your exchange. As I mentioned in the previous section, it is ideal if the decision maker proposes the next step to you. However, this does not always happen. In such cases, it is in your interest to suggest a method of following up to formalize or deepen your discussion, to act on its conclusion:

> May I send you a copy of the memo I prepared?
>
> It would be great to discuss this in more detail. How can I get on your calendar?
>
> I'd like to introduce you to my colleagues.
>
> To make it easier, I will email you a link to our website.
>
> I know you're busy right now. When would be a good time to follow up?

Whatever the decision maker proposes or agrees to, ensure that you act on it quickly. Elevator pitches are, by their nature, fleeting. And if you wait days or weeks to follow up in the manner you discussed, the decision maker may have already forgotten about you. Indeed, following up promptly implicitly conveys the importance of your interaction but also your reliability. Even in cases where the decision maker appears lukewarm to your ideas or proposals, follow up as promised. The worst-case scenario is a nonresponse or a rejection. You've lost nothing but the time required to write an email or send material. The decision maker may refer you to someone else. And you may be able to stay in touch or return to the thread when you have reconnected unexpectedly in the future.

Pointers

AVOID SLOGANS, TRUISMS, OR HACKNEYED PHRASES IN JUSTIFYING YOUR IDEAS

This is a quick way for the decision maker to think that your ideas are not new or that it is a carefully rehearsed pitch rather than an organic conversation. While it is likely that you have rehearsed the elevator pitch before, you want the respondent to walk away thinking that she or he stumbled upon this brilliant idea that emerged in a chat with someone.

USE FACTS AND LOGIC TO JUSTIFY YOUR IDEAS

Instead of slogans, cite interesting tidbits of knowledge that embody the problem you wish to solve or the opportunity that you want to pursue. Do so in a way that is not pompous or self-aggrandizing but that shows instead that you are genuinely interested in sharing these details with a friend or colleague to gain information. These may be counterintuitive and surprising or may offer hard evidence of trends others have only perceived. Having a few strong statistics committed to memory and a few pithy topic sentences is a good place to start.

DEMONSTRATE YOUR AWARENESS OF THE RESPONDENT'S IDEAS, INTERESTS, OR PREVIOUS WORK

This is not just about flattery; it demonstrates knowledge of the field in question and can serve as a bridge with the decision maker. This is a way to show that you are aware of the respondent's pursuits, to explain why you think the respondent would be interested in your ideas, and to show how your ideas link or can be linked to those of the respondent.

GIVE THE RESPONDENT TIME TO THINK AND RESPOND

If you dominate the exchange with the respondent, it ceases to feel like a conversation. The respondent may feel like he or she is being lectured. In actuality, the respondent's reactions and remarks are valuable cues for how to steer the remainder of your pitch.

DEVELOP A BACKUP PLAN

Because it is an exchange, your conversation can and should resemble a negotiation. Instead of posing ultimatums that ask the respondent to accept or reject your ideas, offer multiple next steps the respondent can consider and choose. This way, the respondent has a sense of ownership over the next steps you take together. If the respondent feels ownership of the next step—as if she or he came up with the idea—she or he is more likely to make a long-term investment and respond to your follow-ups.

ALWAYS SHOW RESPECT FOR YOURSELF AND YOUR RESPONDENT

Ensure that you do not demean your respondent's work or ideas in order to set the stage for your own. Ensure that you do not implicitly insult the respondent's knowledge or awareness by oversimplifying. (At the same time, avoid the use of jargon or technical terms that may be beyond her or his understanding. Strike a balance.) On the other hand, there is no need to be self-deprecating or groveling to earn favor. Show that you take yourself seriously, and your respondent will take you seriously, too.

BE PREPARED

Elevator pitches are not always planned. The opportunity may arise when you least expect it. You may happen to see the respondent by chance, or the respondent may seek you out for another reason. Indeed, even when you do plan the circumstances, they are subject to change and interruption. So you need to be agile and ready with your ideas at any moment. It is also wise to know your respondent's style and approach in advance so that, when you meet, you can adjust the extent of your formality, deference, tone, and angle.

IF YOU DON'T KNOW, SAY SO

While preparation is crucial, it is impossible to prepare for everything. If the decision maker poses a question for which you are not prepared, responding with a rambling, long-winded, unfocused answer is not a good use of time. The decision maker, whose time is precious, will be frustrated, and you will not use her or his time to effectively demonstrate your knowledge. Instead, admit that you need to do further research and that you will be happy to follow up soon with a comprehensive response. This can serve as a natural transition to getting the decision maker's contact information and establishing a concrete next step.

ASK QUESTIONS

If your elevator pitch consists entirely of you talking, you may never know what the decision maker thinks. Preparing a few key questions can keep your respondent engaged and allow you to adjust your pitch according to the decision maker's initial response. According to psychology research, people who ask more questions, particularly follow-up questions, are better liked by their conversation partners.[1]

MAKE REALISTIC DEMANDS

Ensure that the proposed next steps between you and the respondent are sufficiently incremental and low-commitment. Given the fleeting nature of elevator pitches, the respondent will be unlikely to make a significant commitment without having the chance to properly consider the implications or consult colleagues. The examples in this chapter require very little immediate investment and make it hard to say "no."

ANTICIPATE OPPORTUNITIES

By their nature, elevator pitches are unplanned. The individual you are targeting has not set a meeting with you and is not attending your presentation. As discussed, the person likely doesn't even know you. Just because they are spontaneous, however, does not mean you can't anticipate them and prepare your remarks in advance. Before you attend meetings, events, or conferences, see if you can review who else will be in attendance. While you can always reach out via email for a chat, you may be more likely to get your desired meeting with a decision maker by approaching that individual in person. When you visit a company, organization, or institution's offices, consider who else you might have the opportunity to meet before

1. Huang, K., Yeomans, M., Brooks, A. W., Minson, J., & Gino, F. (2017). It doesn't hurt to ask: Question-asking increases liking. *Journal of Personality and Social Psychology*, *113*(3), 430–452.

or after your planned activities. Alternatively, research where the targeted individual is making public remarks or a public appearance: attend and try to approach her or him afterward.

PRACTITIONER

***Paige Reffe** was President Bill Clinton's deputy assistant and director of advance at the White House between 1995 and 1996. In that capacity, he was the principal negotiator with foreign governments regarding all of the president's foreign travels and oversaw the logistics. Before working at the White House, Reffe served with the US Senate, the US Department of Justice, the General Services Administration, and the Office of Management and Budget. He is a trained lawyer and was previously a partner at the law firm of Cutler & Stanfield, LLP. He has received and delivered countless elevator pitches, so I asked him to share his advice about preparing them.*

> Let me start with a story. The love of my life (Debbi) has been working in the HIV/AIDS field since the beginning . . . the early 80s. She was once a young Army doctor, an immunologist, and the Army was mysteriously losing men in Africa, not knowing why or from what. So they sent the junior doctors to be at the forefront and try to figure it out. After discovering what the epidemic was and how it was transmitted, the Army developed a set of actions trying to get this epidemic under control. When many villagers would not follow the proscribed actions, Debbi went to see the village elder about how to get better participation. The village elder sat her down and told her he was about to impart to her one of the greatest answers

to life's questions, an answer that would help her resolve all questions and get the answers and action she needed. She listened closely as he told her: "It's quite simple. You just have to know the person who has the key." Simple, yes, but it is oh so true.

I relate this story because it is an essential element to how I viewed "the elevator pitch" when I was a White House official, traveling the world looking at options for President Clinton when he visited a country.

The leader of the US delegation is the chief of protocol, and as the deputy assistant to the president and director of advance, I was the second in command during these trips. On paper, it was the chief of protocol who appeared to be the most important person to influence the president's schedule, but the insider knew that I was the one who held the key. Just being approached by someone signaled to me that he had done his homework. And I listened in a different, much more positive and constructive way.

Still, my attention span was short, and I expected someone to get his or her thoughts to me in 60 seconds or fewer and to get my attention quickly. The better pitches connected an interest or experience of mine with what was being sought. If they did not find an area of commonality or took more than a minute, I would be polite but stop listening. And for all intents and purposes, the opportunity would be lost.

The other essential element was to have a way to get back in touch with me but not take up my time. Thus, one of the questions you ask must be: Who on your staff can I keep in touch with to continue this conversation? Then you must become a semi-irritant and keep in touch. You walk a fine line but need to show that you are proactive and separate yourself from the rest by first writing a "thank you" note and then keeping in touch with regularity.

My favorite elevator pitch story took place during an official visit to Jerusalem and in an actual elevator. Members of the Muslim and Jewish faiths bury their dead within 24 hours. They don't care who is attending the funeral or at what level; religious laws dictate the time and speed with which funerals happen. So when Yitzhak Rabin was assassinated, we scrambled a team very quickly at the White House to ensure that the president attended the funeral (along with 84 other world leaders). Newt Gingrich was the speaker of the US House of Representatives, and he also attended. (You may remember this was the trip during which the speaker complained ever so loudly that he had to fly at the back of Air Force One.) The Israelis wanted to set up meetings between the speaker and the acting prime minister, but I told them that the meeting needed to take place at the King David Hotel. I would find a place for them to meet, but I could not let the speaker travel separately, or I would lose him and not get him to the plane on time to get home.

At the appropriate time, I gathered all of the participants and took them by elevator to their meeting. While on the elevator, the Israelis were all grumbling in Hebrew. My hunch was that they were complaining because they had to come to the speaker, contrary to the usual protocol for such meetings. Understanding the difficulty I had setting up the meeting and listening to their tone, I decided to enter the conversation in English and make the elevator pitch—once again—why they couldn't leave the King David Hotel. The Israeli delegation inferred I could speak Hebrew and that I had understood everything they had just said. They apologized and then just did what they were told. My fluency in context—not Hebrew—made all the difference. Thus, always knowing where you are and being able to give context to conversation can make a very valuable and powerful difference.

PARAGONS

Elevator pitches are rarely recorded or even witnessed by a third party. They take place as private interactions between two individuals and are often mundane enough that they are unlikely to merit media attention. However, they do make appearances in popular films and television fiction. Aaron Sorkin, the screenwriter and producer, is particularly fond of filming "walk and talk" exchanges, which were among the hallmarks of his show The West Wing. *However, many of these mimic the back and forth of elevator pitches and reveal the challenge of accessing and persuading people with power.*

In his adaptation of Michael Lewis' book Moneyball, *Sorkin depicts the world of baseball general managers, who decide which amateur players to recruit, which free agents to contract, and which players to trade. Oakland Athletics general manager Billy Beane is credited with leading the evolution of player selection from a subculture driven by idiosyncratic hunches to one managed according to advanced statistical metrics. This scene captures an elevator pitch that was solicited by Beane from Peter Brand (a character inspired by Paul DePodesta), a Cleveland Indians underling he encountered in a league meeting.*

(a) 

Script excerpt from *Moneyball* (2011)

Screenplay by Steven Zaillian and Aaron Sorkin

SETTING: CLEVELAND INDIANS CORPORATE OFFICES

Peter sits at his cubicle absorbed in his computer until he notices Billy hovering over him.

BILLY: What did you tell Butch?

PETER: Huh? Oh Bruce? I told him I like Garcia.

BILLY; (beat) Why?

PETER: (beat) Probably for the same reasons you do.

BILLY: Meaning what?

PETER: He's undervalued. You were smart to go after him.

BILLY (long beat): What makes him undervalued? . . .

PETER: Baseball thinking is medieval. It's stuck in the Dark Ages. I have a more scientific view of the game.

BILLY: Keep going, Peter.

PETER: There is an epidemic failure within the game to understand what's really happening. And it leads people who run major league teams to misjudge their players and mismanage their teams. They're still asking the wrong questions. People who run baseball teams still think in terms of buying players. Sorry to say that.

BILLY: Peter, don't apologize for what you believe.

PETER: The goal shouldn't be to buy players, what you want to buy is wins. To buy wins, you buy runs. You're trying to replace Johnny Damon. The Red Sox look at Johnny Damon and they see a star worth seven point five million a year. When I look at Johnny Damon, I see an imperfect understanding of where runs come from.

SUDDEN CUT TO ARCHIVAL VIDEO: The back of Johnny Damon's A's jersey as he walks to the plate to adoring Oakland fans.

PETER V/O: His batting average is ignorable. What matters is his on base percentage . . .

DAMON swings at the first pitch and knocks it into left field for a single. He leads off first—

PETER V/O: . . . which in 2001 was .324. That's 10 points lower than league average, and 17 points lower than Garcia's.

On the next pitch, DAMON takes off for second—

PETER V/O: True, he stole some bases. But attempted steals in general have to succeed

70 percent of the time before they even start to contribute to run totals. In 2001 he cost you runs.

DAMON's tagged out at second.

PETER: He's got a good glove. He's a decent leadoff hitter. He steals bases. But he's not worth the seven point five million Boston is paying him. You're lucky to have him off your payroll, it opens all kinds of interesting possibilities.

BILLY: You read Bill James, Pete?

PETER: Yes. These ideas and this approach to the game aren't all new. In fact, some of them have been around for two decades.

BILLY: If this approach has been around for so long, why isn't anybody in baseball doing them?

PETER: That's a much more difficult question than how to win baseball games. Once you begin to pull at that string, your understanding of the world might begin to unravel.

The elevator door closes.

In this scene, Peter is initially reticent. He was not intending to make an elevator pitch, but, when urged by Billy Beane to do so, he explained his ideas in a succinct and compelling manner that made Beane eager to learn more. He gave an example of one of Beane's players who had just signed a contract with a competitor, Johnny Damon—applying his abstract ideas to a tangible situation Beane was immediately confronting. This made his ideas instantly relevant and offered a clear illustration that exhibited the use of his ideas.

In most other cases, people look forward to and even seek out elevator pitches. They can anticipate them when they attend events or venues where they expect to see powerful people for an informal or formal interaction. A second example comes from the film Working Girl. *Here, screenwriter Kevin Wade depicts the cutthroat world of an investment bank, where a rogue secretary, Tess McGill, impersonates her absent boss to deliver a business pitch to a bank executive. Setting aside that, upon meeting the executive in a board room, Tess realizes she had unknowingly slept with him the night before, Tess must settle her nerves to deliver her proposal to broker a significant acquisition for a major client.*

(b) 

Script from *Working Girl* (1988)

Screenplay by Kevin Wade

SETTING: Board Room

Tess fumbles with the folder. The elastic goes flying across the table, just missing Jack. The contents spill out all over the table. Tess gathers them up frantically. The others slide her papers towards her, smiling politely.

TESS (sheepishly): Briefcase . . . lost . . .

She takes a deep breath, tries a smile, looks around and dives in. Nervously, haltingly. She's never done this before.

TESS: In each of the last three quarters, Trask Electronics has announced plans to acquire a major market television station, each time unsuccessfully. At the same time, they have expended time and money fighting off hostile takeover attempts by two of their Japanese competitors. An acquisition of a radio network would in one fell swoop accomplish two important tasks—give Trask a solid base in broadcasting and, because of FCC regulations forbidding foreign ownership of radio stations, wipe out the threat of the Japanese takeover . . .

Any such proposal would normally require at least a half-hour meeting to discuss it in detail, but, under cinematic time constraints, the screenwriter is forced to provide its gist to the viewer. Signaling the longer meeting, this scene ends up simulating an effective elevator pitch. One can imagine Tess giving the same pitch in a minute-long interaction anywhere. While her proposal is clearly far more complicated and risk-laden, the goal of the elevator pitch is to mobilize interest sufficient to secure a more substantial follow-up. And, of course, Tess and Jack would meet again.

THE WEBSITE AND SOCIAL MEDIA

PRINCIPLES

Reaching Everybody, Everywhere, All the Time

I am an older Millennial. Like other Millennials, I am a product of the digital era. Aside from my book collection, my office is paperless. I type much faster than I write. And I tend to check my mobile device more often than is advised.

However, unlike younger Millennials, I vividly remember a world without the internet and mobile technology. My parents purchased an encyclopedia when I was in grade school. I remember that if you didn't read a book chapter for English class, you had to beg a friend to give you a summary; there were no summaries available online. I designed presentations on transparent slides for overhead projectors. I was once given a Rolodex. And I was an undergraduate student at Harvard when my dormitory's facebook turned into, well, Facebook.

So I am a "bridge." While I am sufficiently fluent in (and dependent on) today's digital lifestyle and therefore never really yearn for the simplicity of an earlier era, I am also more aware of the trade-offs involved when information technology makes older forms of social media obsolete. The trade-offs are almost always:

Quality for quantity
Substance for brevity
Authenticity for control

However, it is important to recognize that these are precisely the trade-offs that antecedent forms of communications media pursued. Broadcast appearances meant you didn't need to show up to deliver an elevator pitch. Blogs meant commentators didn't need to lace their messages through press releases. Each advance was more portable, more rapid, and more tightly controlled by the creator. Online social media and websites represent the next step in this evolution. Access is to everybody, everywhere, all the time.

With these new media forms, the fundamentals for succinct writing that I laid out in Chapter 1 still hold. They are—and have been—the building blocks of written works long and short for a very long time. The current market, in particular, champions products and producers that are able to pack maximum content into minimal space and time. Consider the energy bar, the SmartCar, the Apple Watch. This economy values that which is the most, well, economical.

The written manifestation of this trend—for better and for worse—is the tweet. Tweets—along with Instagrams (a.k.a. "grams"), Snapchats ("snaps"), YouTube, and Facebook posts, to a certain extent—are energy bars in the world of knowledge. They help to distill the main idea from a television interview, the storyline of a ballgame, the gist of a government report into bite-sized quantities. Tweets are

SmartCars in a world of information. They can squeeze into the tightest opening in a busy schedule. Tweets are Apple Watches in the world of debate. They are tools that make multiple viewpoints portable for rapid consideration.

That anything important, profound or sophisticated can be communicated in so few words is questionable. However, great rewards await individuals who can succinctly persuade readers. As Chapter 9 will discuss, the question is not which medium is better but rather which medium is more appropriate for the audience you want to reach—for the goals you want to achieve.

Always On

The upside and downside of online social media is that it cannot really be turned off. On the upside, readers, viewers, and audiences can access your ideas at any time of day, any day of the year, from almost anywhere on Earth. On the downside, easy access to information has contributed to a voracious, unceasing appetite for content. To gain a following on social media, it is not simply a matter of posting a few pearls of wisdom: you must do so regularly, engaging followers along the way. And unlike the communications media we discussed earlier, the followers of social media and websites are less predictable. Indeed, because the internet is always "on," you must be too.

Building and maintaining a following represents an investment of all that time "on." Larger and more influential followings act like multipliers. When you tweet, Instagram, Snapchat, and post your ideas to YouTube and Facebook, you build a list of subscribers who are notified about each new post and publication—amplifying your reach. Indeed, people who have amassed enormous followings—called "influencers"—now charge fees to advertisers for access to these followings. The way periodicals and broadcast networks charge for newsprint and 30-second blocks, influencers provide compelling content for free or for very little cost because the magnitude of their subscription base is worth more than any fees they could reasonably charge subscribers to access the content. Most of us do not have the time or inclination to be influencers, but we can emulate their success with our social media presence and our websites.

Twitter champions the skills of elite headline writers from tabloid newspapers, a group of underappreciated professionals who have experienced a renaissance as news media have shifted to online and mobile platforms. Readers now decide what they wish to read and watch during their precious disposable time by quickly—according to market research, extremely quickly[1]—scanning these headlines. The superficiality of readers' decisions has led to the creation of an art: "click bait." Writing pithy, attractive click bait can turn a post by a little-known voice into a movement, a photograph into a campaign.

While many tweeters use the platform to vent, share personal news, or entertain their friends, the master tweeter moves beyond snarky remarks and purposefully connects to a broader or more complex agenda. The master tweeter tempts subscribers with nuggets of text that often link to unseen articles, chats, or imagery. Even when they don't

1. Pernice, Kara (2017). F-shaped pattern of reading on the web: Misunderstood, but still relevant (even on mobile). Nielsen Norman Group, November 12, Retrieved from https://www.nngroup.com/articles/f-shaped-pattern-reading-web-content/

explicitly provide links, tweets rehearse, test, or reinforce a message elaborated elsewhere. Like good topic sentences, good tweets are invitations to read on.

> This photo will change your mind about refugees.
>
> Take five minutes to guarantee fifty years of clean air.
>
> I used to believe in the death penalty, until I read this.
>
> What is the best way to govern in a global pandemic?

Relative to the other media discussed in this book, Twitter, Instagram, etc. all represent an extreme. They are so reductionist that users have no opportunity to truly substantiate their ideas. However, that is not their purpose; their purpose is to stimulate ideas and direct readers to further content. At its worst, of course, Twitter is a megaphone for people to baselessly opine on subjects about which they know very little. But at its best, Twitter offers novel nuggets of information and commentary from experts and thoughtful observers who are able to connect their more substantive analyses to fleeting trends and current affairs.

Consequently, it is worth emphasizing that a well-written tweet cannot be the foundation for a well-written analysis or agenda. Rather, a well-written analysis—structured by strong topic sentences—is required before you can construct a well-written tweet. Indeed, a topic sentence can usually be repurposed *as* a tweet. And like good topic sentences, they beg further substantiation. And the best place to direct people is often to a website with content and archives yo

manage.

The brilliance of websites is that they provide on-dema

content *without* subscription pressures. They are destinat

for those interested in your work and your ideas. In many ways, a well-built website can serve multiple interests at once; and these days, there are many free online templates you can use. An effective website offers a single destination for multiple expressions of your ideas, where visitors may access archives of your tweets, broadcast appearances, briefing slides, publications, op-eds, or blogs. Its organizational logic and styling can convey the way you understand your work and agenda. And its home page can engage with that which is current to draw visitors in further. So for what it lacks in immediate access to viewers, it compensates with depth, versatility, and availability.

Pointers

There are now countless manuals and books that advise on how to create a top-notch website and how to build your social media presence. For the purposes of this book, I want to emphasize a few pointers to complement these existing sources of guidance.

CONTROL YOUR ONLINE PRESENCE

e first step toward building an online presence is always to t some control over it. Type your name or the name of ovement, organization or subject matter into popular gines. What emerges? What does it conceal or prohat you would like people to see? Opening social s and constructing a website allow you to gain ver this impression. This is particularly imave reached a point in your career when seek you out for your expertise or to learn about your portfolio of work (however big or small). A few important steps: choose a relevant, simple web domain or social media handle. (For example, my personal website is JustinGest.com but it funnels to a website hosted by my university.) Ensure that other influencers and other sites point to that domain name and handle. Put it on your business card and in the signature line of your email account. Then use other established techniques for search engine optimization and drive online traffic your way. You may also like to install plug-ins to your website that monitor and analyze traffic.

BE DISCIPLINED

One of the greatest advantages of websites and social media is that you are rendered so much control over what you post. There are no editors, producers, or interlocutors. That means that you need to be your own filter because these profiles should still be carefully curated—more like a library or museum than a refrigerator door or bulletin board. Indeed, because they are reflections of you and impossible to recall, your posts should be high-quality and up-to-date. Also, consider your goal. Is it to sell books? To build a following? To get a job? This will determine what works and the content you wish to post. There is no pressure to be comprehensive.

ESTABLISH AN ORGANIZATIONAL FLOW

Like topic sentences, websites and social media are invitations. The question is, an invitation to what? In what direction are you pushing your visitors, your viewers, and your followers? For example, carefully consider what is in your website menu bar. Evaluate the goals of the sites in the table.

A	*B*	*C*	*D*
Address	About	Biography	Résumé
Hours	Services	Publications	Reports
Gallery	Testimonials	In the news	Order cookies
Events	Consultations	Register for updates	Horoscope

The goal of site A is to attract in-person visits, likely to a brick-and-mortar venue. The goal of site B is to recruit a clientele, likely for services. The goal of site C is to establish a profile, to demonstrate qualifications and build a following. Site D is clearly less focused. Its originator may well write impactful reports, sell delicious cookies, and provide accurate horoscopes. However, each merits its own site with its own logic and flow. Clarity of site often suggests clarity of mind.

WHITE SPACE

Much like newspaper and magazine layouts, much goes into webpage layout and design. The first challenge is to draw the reader in. The second challenge is to maximize space, without overcrowding such that important content is lost in the clutter. For both purposes, white space is key. "White space" refers to space that is unoccupied by text or image. It does not have to be white, but it probably should be to maximize contrast. A luxury of space around the margins, between sections, beneath and above photographs and captions—it all focuses the reader's attention on your content and makes for leisurely reading. It instantly makes the design look clean and crisp. Look at some of the world's best English-language news publications—*The New York Times*, *The Guardian*, *The Washington Post*, *The Economist*. Filled with enormous amounts of content on a daily basis, and given that researchers have found that readers judge websites in as little as 50 milliseconds,[2] it's little wonder that their websites have all started to look much the same.

COME TO LIFE

After spending a long period of time exerting effort to understand a subject matter, it is often a challenge to communicate the compelling relevance of this work with the general public. Websites and social media accounts offer a multimedia extravaganza for doing this. Post videos of yourself discussing your expertise. Many people prefer to learn visually than from reading. Complement headings with vivid photography. Use news pegs to demonstrate relevance. Ask questions that your work addresses.

NEXT STEPS BETWEEN US

As with elevator pitches, ensure that there are ways for followers or visitors to advance their relationship with you in the ways you desire. Provide ways that people can download a copy of your analysis, email you directly, sign up for your newsletter, or buy a copy of your book. Perhaps even offer a discount. This outlet should not be hidden but rather visible and easy to use.

BE MOBILE-FRIENDLY

For websites, ensure that the design platform you select is adapted for mobile viewing. Today, more internet

2. Lindgaard, G., Fernandes, G. J., Dudek, C., & Brown J. (2006). Attention web designers: You have 50 milliseconds to make a good first impression! *Behaviour & Information Technology*, 25, 115–126.

usage is undertaken from mobile devices than traditional computers and laptops. If your website is not easily navigated or viewed from a mobile device, it might as well not exist. It is increasingly easy to craft a multiplatform website. Simply use a service that features "responsive web design," which uses flexible percentage-based sizing to adapt all content to the frame applied. Furthermore, mobile devices make content very easy to share. If you want your work and ideas passed on, embed widgets that permit viewers to share on Twitter, Instagram, Snapchat, and Facebook with ease.

PRACTITIONER

***Jonathan Capehart** is a member of* The Washington Post *editorial board and a regular columnist. He is also a regular contributor to MSNBC, where his commentary focuses on the politics of race, sexuality, and social change. Previously, he wrote for the* New York Daily News, *where he was a part of the team that won a Pulitzer Prize for Editorial Writing in 1999. He then worked for Bloomberg News and New York City mayor Michael Bloomberg. He manages a very active Twitter account with around a quarter of a million followers, and he also posts on Instagram and Facebook and hosts a podcast series. I asked him to reflect on the way social media, particularly Twitter, help him advance his ideas and what goes through his mind each time before he posts.*

I use Twitter like I used to scour the news wires when I first started at the *New York Daily News* editorial page in the early

1990s—to keep me on top of what I need to know in real time. My followers are looking to me for the same reason. As a journalist, my first and foremost goal is to inform, educate, and challenge through civil discourse.

As with any community, my online community (Twitter, Facebook, Instagram, etc.) is built on trust. Many understand I'm an opinion writer and, thus, are looking to me to validate their point of view. But many times, I don't. That I challenge them only adds to the trust built between us. Also, communities stay together and grow because of engagement. I "like," comment on, retweet and engage with my audience in multiple ways.

Humor and reflections of your true personality attract people. For instance, folks know that they can come to me for something interesting on race, politics, or sexual orientation. But my live-tweeting a television show like *Scandal* or tweeting out a twirling Wonder Woman or Diana Ross advising everyone to "Have a great day!" draws in people who wouldn't otherwise follow me. It also lets those already onboard know that I have a life and sense of humor.

I don't expect everyone to agree with what I write or tweet, but I expect my followers and readers to express their displeasure or disagreement in a respectful manner. Those who fill my Twitter feed with bigotry are made an example of via "quoted tweet" and then blocked. I retweet the hatred so the people sending it are shamed and so that they and my followers know I won't be cowed. "Clapping back," as the kids call it, in this way—especially humorously—is another way of building a following.

It won't surprise you that I think the best tweeters are the folks who give me all sorts of accurate information or clever takes in 280 or fewer characters. Mediocre tweeters, however, are those who retweet tweets from five hours earlier, even though the information and conversation has long advanced. In short, mediocre tweeters are usually intermittently active and don't pay close attention.

Now, before or while I'm tweeting, I run through a checklist:

Is this appropriate?

Do I really want to say this?

What's the potential blowback, and am I prepared for that blowback?

Is what I'm retweeting truthful and accurate?

Is it appropriate in tone and tenor for what's happening in the larger world?

More importantly, Twitter and Facebook are places where I let followers and others know about what I've written and when I'll be on television or radio. This is basically a social media perpetual motion activity; one feeds another, which feeds another.

This leads to an important question for those who want to dive into social media: how involved do you want to be? Plenty of people join social media platforms just to spectate or stalk others. They rarely, if ever, post anything. They are there to watch the action by following key people important to their work or passions. But if your goal is to grow a following or an audience for your work, then you must be active.

If you are being cautious, there are two further things to keep in mind. First, don't "protect" your tweets. Doing this is understandable with the raw sewage that sluices around Twitter. But none of your tweets can be retweeted, which is a key way of getting your ideas out to people who might not see them otherwise. Be mindful that some people will look to see who follows you to decide whether you're serious enough to follow. Second, don't follow back everyone who follows you. I shy away from following folks who follow as many people who follow them. It just strikes me as a lack of discretion that could fill your Twitter feed with nonsense you'd rather not see or wouldn't see were it not for such a permissive follow-back stance.

When I'm reading others' tweets, especially during times of crisis, I'm careful to only retweet those who are "verified" with the blue check mark and only those who are reporters or relevant to the crisis or conversation of the moment. I stopped following a fellow journalist years ago because her tweets were always being corrected or had what I knew to be wrong information. The larger lesson learned was the realization that none of us can be a trusted source of information if we are retweeting falsehoods. And if I ever fail in this regard, I own up to it, correct the record, apologize, and keep moving.

The most important thing I would add in closing is to have a social media platform that is just for you. For me, that personal platform is Instagram. I post pretty pictures. All political commentary from commenters is immediately deleted. And thankfully, that's been rare.

What I've written is a lot to take in, so here are some handy DOs and DON'Ts to make it a little easier:

DO understand why you're on social media and what you want to get from it.

DO be funny and engaging.

DO be mindful of what you're tweeting and how it fits in with the tenor and tone of

discussion already in progress.

DO be careful when retweeting during crisis/breaking-news events.

DON'T protect your tweets if your goal is to grow a following.

DON'T retweet information from someone you don't know/trust.

DON'T follow as many people who follow you. Exercise some exclusivity. You wouldn't let everyone in your home, would you?

DON'T join Twitter if you're easily offended. It's rough out there.

PARAGONS

For a truly spectacular piece of digital marketing, look no further than a digital marketer's home page. However, not everyone has a home page like Mark Schaefer, a marketing strategy consultant, author of numerous books, and instructor at Rutgers Business School. His home page is utterly powerful. It is clear, well organized, and designed to sell—sell books, sell lectures, sell consultations, sell Mark! It uses the contrast of black and yellow (which naturally attracts the eye), comfortable amounts of white space, and variation in content to keep the reader scrolling without being overwhelmed. There are ample opportunities to follow Mark on various social media platforms. And despite the variety of his services and enterprises, the site is easy to navigate, and the viewer always knows where to click for more details. However, it is worth acknowledging that not everyone can hire a digital marketer to produce such a site. Moreover, some professionals want to communicate more in the way of credibility and balance, and Schaefer's site could be toned down significantly without losing its impact. The full site may be viewed at http://www.businessesgrow.com. *A series of screenshots is below.*

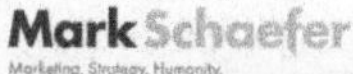

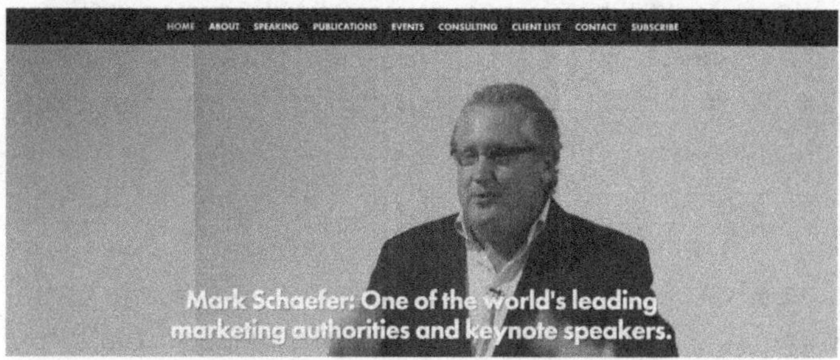

HOME ABOUT SPEAKING PUBLICATIONS EVENTS CONSULTING CLIENT LIST CONTACT SUBSCRIBE

What I do

Audiences LOVE Mark Schaefer's funny and high-energy presentation style. He is the highest- rated speaker in his category. Click here to see examples of his work, examples of speech topics and his current schedule.

Whether a global giant like Adidas or a start-up, companies trust Mark Schaefer for his experience and keen insights. Hire this extraordinary strategist today to get your business on track.

Mark Schaefer has conducted marketing and social media workshops for some of the most recognized brands and organizations in the world. Thousands have enjoyed his entertaining and hands-on approach to education across many industries.

As a contrast, consider the home page of Lynn Vavreck, a professor of political science and communication studies at UCLA and a contributor to The Upshot at The New York Times. *She has authored numerous books and journal articles on political campaigns, elections, and public opinion, including* The Gamble: Choice and Chance in the 2012 Presidential Election *and* The Message Matters: The Economy and Presidential Campaigns. *She manages her own personal website. While I don't endorse some of the aesthetic choices, the pages are exceptionally well organized. The content is fresh, and her list of publications is hyperlinked to PDF editions and booksellers. She features an archive of her contributions to the* New York Times. *This site lacks the charisma and attraction of Mark Schaefer's but suggests greater credibility and focus. Ultimately, Schaefer and Vavreck pursue different things with their communication, and so their sites are designed accordingly. Vavreck's full site may be viewed at www.LynnVavreck.com. A series of screenshots is below.*

Home Publications Books The Upshot SpotCheck About

Sides, John, Chris Tausanovitch, Chris Warshaw, and Lynn Vavreck. 2018. "On the Representativeness of Primary Voters." British Journal of Political Science, March: 1-9.

Sides, John, Michael Tesler, and Lynn Vavreck. 2018. Identity Crisis: The 2016 Presidential Election & the Battle for the Meaning of America, Princeton University Press.

Sides, John, Michael Tesler, and Lynn Vavreck. 2017. "How Trump Lost and Won," Journal of Democracy, 28(2), April, p.34-45.

Sides, John, Michael Tesler, and Lynn Vavreck. 2016. "The Electoral Landscape of 2016," Annals of the American Academy of Political and Social Science, 667, p. 50-71.

Gooch, Andrew A. and Lynn Vavreck. 2016. "How Face-to-Face Interviews and Cognitive Skill affect Item Non-Response: A Randomized Experiment Assigning Mode of Interview," Political Science Research and Methods, 13 June, 1-20.

Paluck, Elizabeth Levy, Paul Lagunes, Donald P. Green, Lynn Vavreck, Limor Peer, and Robin Gomila. 2015. "Does Product Placement Change Television Viewers' Social Behavior," PLOS ONE (September).

Masket, Seth, John Sides, and Lynn Vavreck. 2014. "The Ground Game in 2012: Obama v. Romney," Political Communication 32.

Vavreck, Lynn. 2014. "Want a Better Forecast? Measure the Campaign not just the Economy," PS: Political Science & Politics, April.

Home Publications Books The Upshot SpotCheck About

The Upshot

Independents Approve of the Economy, but Will It Help Republicans in the Midterms?
Relying on independents as a bellwether for political outcomes is not as straightforward as it seems. For one thing, many of them aren't paying that much attention to politics.

Unable to Excite the Base? Moderate Candidates Still Tend to Outdo Extreme Ones
An analysis of more than 30 years of House general elections suggests: Don't nominate someone who will motivate the other side to show up.

Why Asking About Citizenship Could Make the Census Less Accurate
Distrust of the government's intentions toward noncitizens may be hard to overcome, research suggests, and political developments have increased levels of distrust.

Bill Clinton, Roy Moore and the Power of Social Identity
It may feel to Americans that an intense state of us-versus-them is something new, but it's not. People have been using party as a lens to filter information for decades and beyond.

Why Trump's Softening on Immigration Is Unlikely to Splinter His Base

Ian Bremmer is the founder of the political risk advisory firm, Eurasia Group. He has a Stanford PhD, has written ten books, and is a staple on the news networks and in the opinion columns. More importantly for our purposes here, he is social media-savvy. Bremmer's Twitter account represents his jack-of-all-trades nature: some tweets are light-hearted quips, others analytical or thought-provoking. He does an excellent job of communicating in short, punchy statements and is especially fond of lists—which are easy to read quickly and say a lot with very few characters. He also regularly links to the news to market his trademark ideas and concepts—such as the "J-curve" and "GZero." He also seeks opportunities to expand the reach of reports and articles that he or his firm has authored. See the chronologically ordered examples below from an eight-day span in January 2018.

This is as good a time as any to remind you all that there are no tweets in my #TopRisks2018 report: eurasiagroup.net/toprisks2018

> **Donald J. Trump** @realDonaldTrump · Jan 2, 2018
> Crooked Hillary Clinton's top aid, Huma Abedin, has been accused of disregarding basic security protocols. She put Classified Passwords into the hands of foreign agents. Remember sailors pictures on submarine? Jail! Deep State Justice Dept must finally act? Also on Comey & others

7:58 AM · Jan 2, 2018 · Twitter Web Client

13 Retweets **31** Likes

Here, Bremmer satirically employs a tweet by President Trump to publicize an article he wrote enumerating the top political risks of 2018—a classic year-end prospectus published at a time when readers have down time to reflect.

Great piece from Fareed on Iran demonstrations...and a nice nod to how the J curve fits in.

Opinion | Iran has the ingredients for revolution — but a strong regime to ward it off
For now, that means a period of instability.
washingtonpost.com

12:48 PM · Jan 5, 2018 · Twitter Web Client

20 Retweets **66** Likes

Here, Bremmer draws attention to Fareed Zakaria's Washington Post *column, in which Bremmer's ideas are cited.*

I don't believe the US is in decline.
1. Food
2. Energy
3. Technology
4. Higher Education
5. Defense
6. Demographics
7. Geography

But US influence on the global stage is declining rapidly.
1. China
2. Divided Europe
3. Rogue States/Non-State Actors
4. America First

#GZero

3:42 PM · Jan 6, 2018 · Twitter for iPhone

128 Retweets 330 Likes

With a list, Bremmer here pushes back on the growing argument that the United States is in decline and adds nuance: "domestic decline? No. But a decline in international leadership? Yes." He then uses the hashtag #GZero, referring to a term he coined "to denote the absence of a politically and economically dominant country or bloc." By connecting his insight to his broader work, Bremmer keeps his audience engaged while building his intellectual profile.

Typical arrival times, Oval Office

Bush 43 6:45am
Obama 9-10am
Trump 11am

Being President must be getting easier.

10:50 AM · Jan 8, 2018 · Twitter for iPhone

351 Retweets **1.1K** Likes

Here, Bremmer uses humor to provide a unique framework to the popular impression that President Trump works shorter hours than his predecessors.

Every day:

217,000 people rise out of extreme poverty globally

325,000 gain access to electricity,

300,000 to clean drinking water.

7:37 AM · Jan 10, 2018 · Twitter for iPhone

631 Retweets **1.6K** Likes

Here, Bremmer provides a few statistics that are simple yet overwhelming. Because the statistics speak for themselves, Bremmer gets right to the point and does not interfere with heavy-handed analysis.

A MULTIMEDIA STRATEGY

PRINCIPLES

In the first chapter of this book, I emphasized that the more media in which you can fluently communicate your message, the more effective you likely will be. Like languages, the more media you may engage, the more people you may reach. And because different causes and campaigns require different strategies, versatility is valuable. It allows you to adapt to the circumstances and communicate your ideas broadly to the targeted community, strategically in ways that appeal to their worldview, and effectively persuade them to support and advance your ideas. How you develop your communication strategy depends on the answers to three key questions.

Whom Do I Need To Reach?

Policy matters are almost always matters of stasis and change. Whether you are a policymaker, an advocate, or an analyst, you seek ways to improve and develop your society into a more prosperous, virtuous, successful place; and disagreements arise both over how people understand prosperity, virtue, and success as well as over what should be done to promote them. The first question you must ask pertains to what needs to happen to motivate and enact the change you wish to facilitate. This sets off a series of sequential questions:

What policies regulate your specific subject matter?

What institutional body (or bodies) oversees this area of public concern?

How does this body change, implement, or create new policies?

Once you have clarified the policy setting, institutional authority, and its internal dynamics, you come to the enduring fact that these institutions are ultimately constructed and controlled by human beings. Nothing a government does is automatic or random. (Even when the outcomes are as good as random, this is due to a human-made decision to manage a process in such a way that produces these as-good-as-random outcomes.) Accordingly, you need to consider a further set of sequential questions that address the human beings behind the institutional processes you identify as relevant to your work:

Who then are the people who are integral to this process?

Is it one individual who holds arbitrary power?

Is it a panel of people who deliberate?

Is it a chamber of partisan legislators?

Is it a large constituency of voters?

Is it a middle manager or clerk, balancing power inside a bureaucracy?

Who or what influences their decisions?

Is it a large constituency of voters? (The masses)
Is it a select constituency of industry insiders or stakeholders? (The elites)
Is it their own ideology, reason, whim, or relationships? (Arbitrary power)

What Do They Need to Know?

What information and message will most effectively persuade the people you need to reach? Are simple facts or an overview of your findings and arguments sufficient? This may be the case if you're trying to dispel myths, initiate curiosity about a new issue, or inspire new thinking or a change of direction in an established subject matter. Or is persuasion more a matter of communicating the details and nuances involved? This may involve more complicated policy matters or established policy matters that you wish to refine or modify.

What Is the Best Way to Reach Them?

The answer to each of the preceding two questions produces the answer to the third question of which communications medium best suits your agenda. In Figure 9.1, address the questions in the columns from left to right to generate the suggested medium. For example, if you need to reach an individual with arbitrary power and your message is one of nuance, then it is sensible to pursue a briefing with the selected individual and her or his support staff. If you need to make the masses aware of a new issue and your message is more of

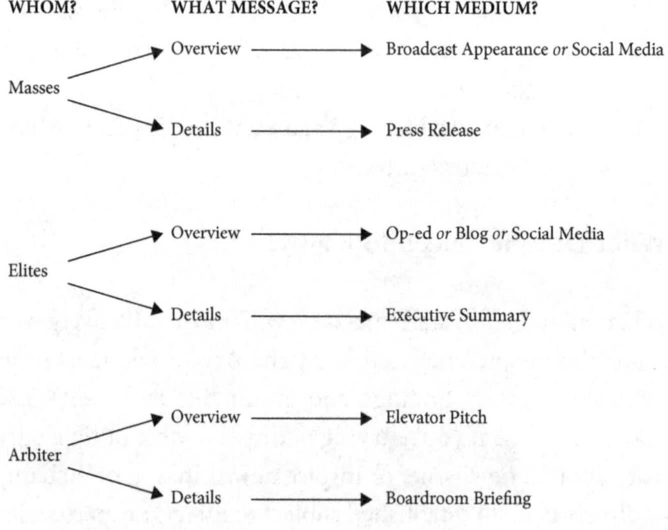

FIGURE 9.1 Strategic Communication Matrix

an introduction, pursue a television or radio appearance or engage with social media.

Note that the answers to the questions I lay out are not necessarily mutually exclusive. A campaign may be well served by outreach to the masses *and* people holding arbitrary power. A campaign may be well served by the effective communication of its ideas in detail *and* overview form. As a result, you may well need to draft a press release, write an op-ed, *and* prepare a briefing. This is a multimedia strategy—but with proper consideration, it will be deliberate and purposeful.

The design of such a multimedia strategy will depend on your job. Researchers seek to inject their findings and ideas into the intellectual bloodstream. Advocacy organizations seek to achieve issue-related goals, whether they relate to public discourse or legislation. Elected officials tend to be more focused on persuading constituents that they should remain in office, but they also pursue policy goals. Just ensure that your choices of communication media are not limited by your proficiencies.

The Evolution of Policy Communication

The technological advances of the 21st century promise sophisticated evolution in the communication of policy ideas. LinkedIn and other professional networking hubs are new venues for elevator pitches. YouTube and other video-posting sites permit broadcast appearances without invitations from guest bookers. Personal blogs similarly facilitate the self-publication of op-eds and news analysis. Moreover, innovations in graphic design and presentation software visually enhance the delivery of briefings, whether in person or via video conference.

If the world of public policy is subject to relationships and cronyism—and it certainly can be—these advances reduce barriers to entry. They remove intermediaries and gatekeepers like producers, editors, and personal schedulers. However, they do not remove the fundamentals of policy communication that this book enumerates. The relevance of these various guidelines endures and may even increase when new, mediating technologies hinder clarity, reduce our capacity to convey charisma in interpersonal communication, and prevent those pesky intermediaries from enforcing fundamentals.

That is the nature of fundamentals; they remain true despite evolutions in taste and technology. And at the core of all these evolving media are words. Continue to choose them carefully and package them in different ways to appeal to different people for different purposes.

AFTERWORD

THE WORLD IS IN A moment of informational instability. Various observers have lamented the proliferation of "fake news" and the rise of "alternative facts" in a "post-truth" environment.

Through the most optimistic lens, the public has become less accepting of the words they read and hear and more critical of authorities—business leaders, officials, and scientists alike. We have become more sensitive to personal bias and aware that its contamination reaches the highest echelons of our societies. We are wary of people's personal agendas and how their desire to influence may be a self-serving attempt to advance their own interests. If everyone is out for herself or himself, it is implicitly thought, we are accountable to no one. This can be a healthy form of skepticism.

Far more pessimistically, sinister influences in our societies have manipulated this skepticism to undermine trust in sources that actually *are* objective and accountable—to certifying agencies, ombudspersons, external evaluation, and peer review. The manipulators have generated conspiracy theories, myths, and faux science that validate people's unfounded suspicions and sustain their convenient truths. And we, the public, are eager accomplices. We limit ourselves to certain information outlets that reinforce our worldviews. Rather than read broadly, we read deeply—if we even read at all. Institutionalized by internet-based software that recognizes these isolating consumption habits and caters to them, different constituencies now occupy different subcultures with competing conventional wisdoms. In this disorienting cacophony, the truth is but one blade of grass indistinguishable in a field of green.

One such convenient truth is that scientists, experts, and authorities are the innocent victims of these insidious developments that undermine the impact of our investigations and findings.

To the contrary, scientists, experts, and authorities played a role in making this world; and they have a role to play in unmaking it.

Indeed, a principal reason for the indistinguishable nature of expertise is that we experts have done little to publicize our methods and ideas to the mainstream public and its decision makers. We assign value exclusively to the publication of scientifically derived facts in highly specialized journal publications, which are often written in a manner illegible to even an informed layperson and then hidden behind an intimidating pay-wall. We have so specialized into narrow subfields that we are unable to speak across them. The "death of expertise" has been one of self-inflicted wounds.

Meanwhile, the creators of "alternative facts" and "fake news" succinctly package their ideas into slick videos and campaigns with clear formatting and persuasive prose that is accessible to all. In this world of influence, there is no pay-wall, no jargon, and no impact without breadth.

Thus, the broad-minded share their ideas narrowly, while the narrow-minded share their ideas broadly.

To remedy this paradox and restore a society that recognizes truth, we must complement the generation of new knowledge with its impactful dissemination. We must value and pursue multimedia outreach to connect with voters and decision makers who hold the authority to craft societies informed by science and fact.

This does not mean that we must abandon conventional means of peer review and dissemination to other experts in our respective fields. Rather, it means that we must recognize that these conventional outlets are insufficient and not conducive to mass appeal.

Just as new developments in scientific methods and knowledge require us to adapt our skill set, this new moment of informational instability requires us to find new ways to distinguish our work and persuade our fellow citizens of its use.

Should we choose not to, we have only ourselves to blame.

SOURCES CITED

Alinsky, S. (1990). *Rules for radicals: A practical primer for realistic radicals*. New York: Vintage Books.

Huang, K., Yeomans, M., Brooks, A. W., Minson, J., & Gino, F. (2017). It doesn't hurt to ask: Question-asking increases liking. *Journal of Personality and Social Psychology, 113*(3), 430–452.

Iyengar, S., & Kinder, D. R. (2010). *News that matters: Television and American opinion*. Chicago, IL: University of Chicago Press.

Jamali, H. R., & Nikzad, M. (2011). Article title type and its relation with the number of downloads and citations. *Scientometrics, 88*(2), 653–661.

Jamieson, K. (2015). Communicating the value and values of science. *Issues in Science and Technology, 32*(1), 72–79. Retrieved from http://www.jstor.org.ezp-prod1.hul.harvard.edu/stable/24727008

Kahneman, D., & Anderson, Norman B. (2003). A perspective on judgment and choice. *American Psychologist, 58*(9), 697–720.

Lakoff, George. (2008). *The political mind: Why you can't understand 21st-century politics with an 18th-century brain*. New York, NY: Penguin.

Letchford, A., Moat, H. S., & Preis, T. (2015). The advantage of short paper titles. *Royal Society Open Science*, 2, 150266. Retrieved from http://dx.doi.org/10.1098/rsos.150266

Lindgaard, G., Fernandes, G. J., Dudek, C., & Brown J. (2006). Attention web designers: You have 50 milliseconds to make a good first impression! *Behaviour & Information Technology, 25*, 115–126.

Luntz, F. (2007). *Words that work: It's not what you say, It's what people hear*. New York, NY: Hachette Books.

Maoz, I., Ward, A., Katz, M., & Ross, L. (2002). Reactive devaluation of an "Israeli" vs. "Palestinian" peace proposal. *Journal of Conflict Resolution*, *46*(4), 515–546.

McNeil, B. J., Pauker, S. G., Sox, H. C., & Tversky, A. (1982). On the elicitation of preferences for alternative therapies. *New England Journal of Medicine*, *306*, 1259–1262.

Newman, N., Fletcher, R., Levy, D., & Nielsen R. (2016). *Reuters Institute digital news report 2016*. Oxford, UK: Reuters Institute for the Study of Journalism.

Pernice, Kara. (2017). F-shaped pattern of reading on the web: Misunderstood, but still relevant (even on mobile). Nielsen Norman Group, November 12. Retrieved from https://www.nngroup.com/articles/f-shaped-pattern-reading-web-content/

Quattrone, G., & Tversky, A. (1988). Contrasting rational and psychological analyses of political choice. *American Political Science Review*, *82*(3), 719–736. doi:10.2307/1962487

Sehgal, K. (2016). How to write email with military precision. *Harvard Business Review*, November 22. Retrieved from https://hbr.org/2016/11/how-to-write-email-with-military-precision

Steinmetz, J., Xu, Q., Fishbach, A., & Zhang, Y. (2016). Being observed magnifies action. *Journal of Personality and Social Psychology*, *111*(6), 852–865. Retrieved from http://dx.doi.org/10.1037/pspi0000065

Stephens, B. (2017). Tips for aspiring op-ed writers. *New York Times*, August 25.

Strunk, W., & White, E. B. (2000). *The elements of style* (fourth edition). New York, NY: Pearson Longman.

Tigue, C. C., Borak, D. J., O'Connor, J. J., Schandl, C., & Feinberg, D. R. (2012). Voice pitch influences voting behavior. *Evolution and Human Behavior*, *33*(3), 210–216.

Tversky, A., Kahneman, D., & Hoffman, Martin L. (1983). Extensional versus intuitive reasoning: The conjunction fallacy in probability judgment. *Psychological Review*, *90*(4), 293–315.

Westen, D. (2007). *The political brain: The role of emotion in deciding the fate of the nation*. New York, NY: Public Affairs.

Willis, J., & Todorov, A. (2006). First impressions: Making up your mind after a 100-ms exposure to a face. *Psychological Science*, *17*(7), 592–598.

INDEX